MORE THAN JUST A GAME

Praise for *More Than Just a Game*

"An engagingly written, invaluable overview of the contemporary youth sports landscape and how it developed. *More Than Just a Game* offers an exceptional blend of insights from previous research, new original research findings, and assorted personal stories, observations, and analyses. It helps to illuminate what often appears to be a mystifying, arbitrary, expensive, and inefficient youth sports delivery system. It offers a fair assessment of the costs and benefits of how things are working and very well-informed suggestions for how to improve youth sports experiences. A major contribution!"

Chris Knoester, PhD, Professor of Sociology, The Ohio State University

• • •

"*More Than Just a Game* offers an insightful ethnography into the modern American youth sport 'society.' Through systematic interviews and observation, Chris Bjork and William Hoynes expose some of the deepest-held myths about youth sport participation and how these myths may be damaging kids and families. The book's underlying message should be taken seriously: parents should not betray their kids' childhood fun with misinformed dreams about college scholarships, by viewing youth sport success as evidence of good parenting, and by trying to keep up with those in their 'mobile youth sport communities.' Kids, not parents, should drive youth sport participation (or nonparticipation)."

Rick Eckstein, PhD, Professor of Sociology, Villanova University, Author of *How College Athletics Are Hurting Girls' Sports: The Pay to Play Pipeline,* Coproducer and research director of the documentary series, *Beyond Stigma: Mental Health in Women's College Sports*

• • •

"*More Than Just a Game* goes into the dynamic aspects of youth sports that has become a culture of high specificity and high commitment. This is a common motif in American culture at large, with Bjork and Hoynes providing valuable insights as to how it has impacted the lives of so many young athletes and their families. If we want to change the culture at large, to reduce injuries and burdens while maximizing what is best for the kids, we must first become self-aware of the benefits and drawbacks. This book is the perfect way to pioneer that discussion."

Christian Hilts, PT, DPT, OCS, CSCS

"You'll not find a better analysis of the child sports industry or guidebook for navigating your kids through youth sports than this perceptive, comprehensive, and very readable book by Bjork and Hoynes. Reflecting the transition from child-centered sandlots to adult-controlled firms and institutions, and from community-based teams/leagues to private clubs/leagues, *More Than Just a Game* examines sports commercialization, the travel ball craze and its inequities, youth-sports power struggles, the illusion of college sports, and their implications for beleaguered young athletes and their parents. Filled with insights and good advice for those involved in the next generation of youth sports."

Robert Elias, Author of *Major League Rebels, The Empire Strikes Out,* and *Baseball and the American Dream*

• • •

"This book is an exceptional resource for parents of current and aspiring youth athletes to understand the broader context surrounding youth sports, the business of youth sports, and intersections between today's youth sports industry, schools, and colleges. It is an equally essential resource for those working in academic institutions, especially in selective postsecondary institutions at whatever level of the collegiate-athletics hierarchy."

Bruce D. Baker, EdD, Professor, Department of Teaching and Learning, University of Miami

• • •

"*More Than Just a Game* is a clear-eyed, highly readable analysis of contemporary youth sports, as well as an insightful account of what organized kids' athletics means to parents. Grounded in original research, the book avoids pat explanations for parents' behavior and always finds the nuance in their motivations and conduct. The authors are relentlessly fair, and their suggestions on how to navigate the ever-changing sports environment are essential. Parents, if you are confused about travel T-ball, year-round soccer for second graders, and why kids' games cost so much—read this book!"

Linda Flanagan, Freelance Writer, Former High School Coach, Author of *Take Back the Game: How Money and Mania Are Ruining Kids' Sports—and Why It Matters*

• • •

"An essential read for any parents wondering where their weekends went—as well as whether such a thing as leisure exists anymore. A compelling, clear-eyed look at the changing norms around youth sports, family, and what it means for us to spend meaningful time together."

Hua Hsu, Pulitzer Prize-winning author of *Stay True: A Memoir*

CHRIS BJORK · WILLIAM HOYNES

MORE THAN JUST A GAME

HOW THE YOUTH SPORTS INDUSTRY IS CHANGING THE WAY WE PARENT AND WHAT TO DO ABOUT IT

CRP
CENTRAL RECOVERY PRESS

LAS VEGAS, NV

Central Recovery Press (CRP) is committed to publishing exceptional materials addressing addiction treatment, recovery, and behavioral healthcare topics.

For more information, visit www.centralrecoverypress.com.

Publisher: Central Recovery Press
530 S 6th Street
Las Vegas, NV 89101

30 29 28 27 26 25   1 2 3 4 5

Library of Congress Cataloging-in-Publication Data has been applied for.

Photo of Chris Bjork by John Abbott/Vassar College. Photo of William Hoynes by Karl Rabe/Vassar College.

Publisher's Note
This book contains general information about practical strategies on how parents can learn to navigate the youth sports system that frequently ignores the needs of kids. The information contained herein is not medical advice. This book is not an alternative to medical advice from your doctor or other professional healthcare provider.

Our books represent the experiences and opinions of their authors only. Every effort has been made to ensure that events, institutions, and statistics presented in our books as facts are accurate and up to date. To protect their privacy, the names of some of the people, places, and institutions in this book may have been changed.

Cover design by The Book Designers. Interior design by Sara Streifel, Think Creative Design.

To our families
Etsuko, Kai, and Cory (Chris)
Deirdre, Ben, and Nick (William)

essential sources of learning and joy

CONTENTS

PREFACE

If you picked up this book, chances are you are a parent, family member, friend, or coach of a young athlete. You want to help that person find enjoyment and success through sports but aren't sure how to do that. Bombarded with news reports that highlight the troubling parts of the youth sports world—coaches who berate their players, parents who lose control at athletic competitions, kids who experience debilitating pressure, a rash of injuries among teen athletes—you may be curious, and confused, about what happened to kids' sports.

At the same time, you probably also know that sports can help kids develop confidence and skills that will help them throughout their lives. Perhaps you, or one of your family members, played competitive sports at some point in the past. So you know playing on a team with a group of motivated individuals can be a richly rewarding experience, full of challenges and opportunities for personal growth and collective bonding. Even if you didn't play sports, you probably know from experience what it's like to be part of a team. At some point in your life, you've played on a team knitted together by a shared commitment to a collective task: on a youth sports club as a kid, a rock band or theater group, a volunteer effort in your community, or as part of a project team at your job. Regardless of what your team accomplished, you have fond memories of the friends you made through team activities. Being part of a team, both the challenges you faced and the connections you made, likely helped you develop into the person you are today.

If you are a parent, you probably want your child to have meaningful team experiences, but it's hard to know what type of support you should provide. Regardless of whether you were a youth athlete yourself, you'll likely find that, as with so many parenting challenges in the age of always-on social media, things seem so different than when you were a child. The rules have changed. The stakes have increased. Kids experience different expectations and new kinds of pressure. It's no surprise that so many parents go through profound uncertainty about how they can help their children participate in sports without being overwhelmed by the toxic parts of the youth sports industry.

We understand where you're coming from. When our children were younger, we weren't sure what roles we should play in their extracurricular activities. We both played sports as kids, but that didn't prepare us very well for becoming youth sports parents. During our childhood, parents weren't expected to center their lives around their kids' practices and games. Sports careers were to be observed, not managed.

By the time we became parents, expectations had shifted, and we struggled to understand the new norms. We wanted to support our kids without putting excessive pressure on them. If we took a more hands-off approach, though, would our children lose opportunities to kids with more assertive parents? Would we miss a valuable opportunity to connect with our children? Should we be more active in advocating for our children? Should we sign up our kids for a "travel team," something we didn't know much about, instead of a local recreational program? We weren't sure how to strike the appropriate balance. What's more, we didn't know where to get the information we needed to make sound decisions for our kids and our families. We stumbled along, guided by instinct rather than expertise or careful planning.

Years later, as the two of us shared stories about our experiences as parents of young athletes, we commiserated about how little information was available to people like us. Even the most well-intentioned parents seemed to be often in the dark as they made decisions for their kids. Figuring out who to turn to for support or where to find relevant information was, and continues to be, a real challenge.

That realization was the impetus for us to write this book. We hoped to provide information for parents and others that would help them make sense of the current world of youth sports. Our own children are grown now, well into their adult lives, and their playing days ended several years ago. Still, we continue to hear from friends, neighbors, and colleagues who have the same kinds of questions we had as they struggle to navigate the perplexing youth sports scene. We wanted to offer parents the information they needed to make decisions that would fit the long-term goals they had for their children, both on and off the sports field.

Motivated by that goal, we have spent much of the last ten years studying the youth sports industry. We spoke to as many people as we could—players, coaches, referees, and parents—to obtain their perspectives on youth athletics. First, we followed a handful of local youth sports teams, attending their practices and games, traveling with them to tournaments, and observing team meetings. We thought those activities would complement our own experiences, because as parents of young athletes it can difficult to evaluate things dispassionately. After that, we sought out parents and coaches from different parts of the country. We asked adults from California to Florida to reflect on how children benefit from playing sports and what they think needs to be changed. What do they wish they had known when their children started playing? What advice would they give to other parents? Those conversations tended to last much longer than we had anticipated. Most of the adults we spoke to were eager to share their thoughts about youth sports. Driving many of their comments was a desire to help other parents negotiate what many found to be an opaque and confusing system. In the chapters that follow, we share those insights, including many excerpts from our interviews, using pseudonyms for all of the parent, coach, and player names throughout the book.

Although each of us has written academic books before, we wrote this book with the aim of reaching a broader audience. From the early days of developing a road map for this project, our focus has remained squarely on the parents, family members, and friends of young athletes who are struggling to do what's best for those kids. We hope to help them make decisions with a sense of the big picture—of how the youth sports industry is organized— as well as the implications of the seemingly minor choices they make for children. In other words, we wrote the book we wish had been available when our kids first signed up to play sports.

Chris Bjork and William Hoynes
September 2024

Sports, Success, and Parenting

The sports industry seems to have grabbed hold of American culture like no other institution. It shapes the lives of individuals, drives social trends, and anchors community life in many locations. How can it be that the football coach at the university of Michigan earns a salary 225 times greater than that of the President of the United States? When children are asked to name their heroes, they are more likely to refer to a sports star than a teacher, business leader, or government official. And the amount Americans devote to athletics—playing, watching, or betting on—seems to be steadily increasing. In contemporary society, sports fans can follow their favorite team around the clock, on television, online, or through social media.

In this book, we examine the contours of the complex youth sports landscape, offering a window onto current debates surrounding an industry rampant with myths and misinformation. Our experience tells us that we cannot understand, let alone reform, youth sports if we don't look honestly at how and why kids' sports matter so much to so many participants.

In our current climate of concern about the state of youth sports, understanding how children and adults navigate this intense world has become an urgent task. Why have families been so eager to invest so much time, effort, and money in their children's athletic careers? What are the consequences of centering the life of youngsters on sports? How can parents best look out for their kids, given the values that currently shape the decisions they make?

We were motivated to explore these questions as parents and as researchers. We both have been involved in youth sports for more than a decade. When our children first joined sports teams, we had no idea what we were getting into. The world of youth sports had undergone extensive changes since we were kids. Faced with uncertainty, we asked our friends for advice and followed their lead. Over the years, we became more familiar with the ins and outs of the business. As coaches and board members, we had opportunities to look behind the curtain—to observe how teams were formed, the politics of running a league, the financial costs associated with youth sports, and experiences of young athletes.

Despite this exposure to youth athletics, both of us felt that our understanding of the youth sports world was rather narrow. Most of the reports about youth sports we read offered one-sided stories, either portraying participants as obsessively pursuing unrealistic dreams or valiantly helping their kids achieve success. Such simplistic accounts failed to capture the realities of youth sports. In our experiences, most parents made decisions about their children's athletic activities without a clear sense of how those decisions fit into any long-term goals they had.

Motivated to develop a more nuanced understanding of this topic, we designed a research project that focused on the world of competitive youth sports today. Over a period of two years, we followed four travel teams, observing practice sessions, chatting with participants, and traveling to tournaments with the teams. In addition, we surveyed more than 500 parents. This survey asked respondents to share their views about a wide range of topics related to youth sports, such as the amount of time and money they spent on their children's athletic activities, their level of satisfaction with travel sports, and the goals they had for their children.

As we started to reflect on the information we had collected, we were struck by a stark disconnect between parents' opinions about youth sports and the realities of that industry. That mismatch was leading many adults to make decisions that were not always in their children's best interests. Before their children had entered their teens, parents were being encouraged to sign up their children to play for elite teams that played year-round. And the longer they continued playing sports, the more powerful the pressure to specialize became.

Although some of the issues described above had received attention in the popular media, we found those reports tended to highlight extreme behavior. This makes sense, given the pressure journalists feel to sell newspapers and attract followers. Free from those pressures, we designed a project that would capture the realities of parents today. We wanted to learn as much as we could about their experiences, both positive and negative. Recognizing the enormity of this task, we decided to focus on a handful of general themes:

1. Goals for Children

People make all sorts of assumptions about why parents encourage their children to play organized sports. Few take the time to speak with them in-depth about the thinking that goes into this decision. We were eager to discover more about how the decisions affected their families, their relationships with their children, and their views about parenting. Anchoring all of these conversations was the basic question, "What do you hope to get out of this experience?"

As they reflected on this question, the parents we spoke with seemed to be expressing ideas that were still muddled in their minds. Many remarked that they hadn't initially given this decision a great deal of thought. They just followed the wishes of their child or the lead of another parent. Even adults whose children had been playing sports for years often struggled to express their thoughts precisely. Their comments underscored how challenging it can be for parents to oversee their children's development in a system that transmits strong yet inconsistent messages about the reasons for playing sports.

2. Levels of Involvement

The topic of sports parents often stirs up images of unhinged adults who will do whatever it takes to help their children get ahead. We tried to dig beneath the surface of this stereotype to develop a more accurate understanding of sports parents. As we conducted our interviews, we sought to understand in concrete terms the roles they played in shaping their children's athletic careers. During those conversations, we asked mothers and fathers to think carefully about the amount of time they invested in sports-related activities. We also encouraged them to reflect on their connections to teams, how the decisions they made influenced their children's attitudes toward sports, and the ways their involvement shifted over time.

3. Views about Winning

The youth sports industry has become more intense and commercial in recent years. We were curious to learn how adults raised in a different era are responding to current views about competition and winning. How are they negotiating the tensions between the traditional ideal of playing sports for fun and the current pressure to outperform other athletes? How are their decisions affecting their children's experiences on and off the playing field?

To get a better sense of parents' thoughts about this topic, we posed a series of questions related to winning and athletic performance. Their reflections were invaluable to us when we attended practices, games, and tournaments. At those events, we compared the views expressed by parents with their actual behavior in the stands. We were curious to see when parents followed through on their stated values related to winning and when their behavior clashed with those ideals. Throughout our period of research, we tried to incorporate these multiple perspectives on youth sports to come up with more complete explanations of parent behavior.

4. Positive and Negative Aspects of Youth Sports

Although reporters sometimes interview parents about the individual accomplishments of their children, they often focus on their reactions to immediate events. Away from the playing field, distanced from the emotionally charged atmosphere of an important game, we asked parents to reflect on their experiences with youth sports. Because the teams we focused on were composed primarily of high school students, most of their parents had been overseeing their athletic careers for six or seven years. Almost all of their children had played on multiple teams, for several different coaches. This provided them with a depth of experience that proved valuable when they spoke about the goals and structure of the entire system. Those comments were extremely useful to us as we attempted to fit together all the puzzle pieces we had collected.

The Bigger Picture

Studying a handful of sports teams closely helped us understand the challenges that confront young athletes and their families today. As researchers, we could reflect on the reasons parents made certain decisions for their kids and the impact of those decisions with a sense of distance that wasn't available to us when our own kids were playing sports and we were so emotionally invested in their activities. That sense of separation allowed us to identify patterns in parent behavior that we might not have noticed if we had been active participants in team activities.

Studying youth sports teams also gave us fresh perspectives on the society in which we live. Parents did not make decisions in isolation. As they managed their children's athletic careers, they were affected, sometimes consciously and sometimes unknowingly, by recent shifts in their communities. To truly understand the decisions parents made, we had to think about the ways their behavior was affected by economic, technological, social, and demographic influences. Adults made individual decisions, but they operated within systems that had a powerful influence on their behavior. Reports on youth sports tend to overlook that critical component of the story.

As we pushed ourselves to think more deeply about the stories people told us, we came to appreciate their attempts to create stability and purpose in the face of great uncertainty. We discovered that although adults made decisions about sports with their children's needs in mind, they often benefited from travel sports in ways they hadn't anticipated. The connections they formed with other parents provided them with a sort of social stability that was missing in their lives. In previous generations, adults tended to form close relationships with their neighbors. Schools and neighborhoods formed the center of their social lives. That is rarely the case today. We spend less time talking with our friends in person and more time exchanging messages with them online. This can reduce the social pressures parents experience but can also lessen their sense of social connection. As a result, many of the parents we interviewed came to rely on other team families for support.

The decisions parents made about their children's athletic activities are also tied to recent shifts in the structure of play in our society. Children today spend less time playing with kids in their neighborhoods. Free exploration has been replaced by scheduled activities. And when they do have free time, children tend to rely on electronic devices to keep them occupied. As Professor of Neuroscience Eric Leuthardt has written, "When I was a kid I used to dig holes in the backyard for fun. Now I see children the same age as my hole-digging days navigating the web through wirelessly connected smartphones and getting weepy when their transfer rates are too slow. Beyond this underlining of my age, it also speaks to the fact that life as we knew it back then was very different from what it is now." The changes described by Leuthardt have created a void in the lives of children that many parents are constantly trying to fill. Should we be surprised when they decide to sign up their kids to play for a team that practices several times a week, all-year-round?

Parents do not exist in a vacuum. They make decisions in response to a multitude of forces, some of which even they do not recognize. To truly understand the challenges associated with mentoring young athletes today, it is essential to connect the actions of their parents to broader trends and influences. If we do this thoughtfully, the insights generated can produce a much richer account of youth sports than is provided in most newspaper articles or television reports.

Broader Significance

Parents today are trying to do what they think is best for their children. This isn't always easy. In many cases, making sure your kids are safe and happy is no longer considered enough. Books, news stories, and social media all convey to parents the notion that they should do whatever they can to make sure their children are exceptional. The barrage of photos that appear in their daily Instagram feed alone is enough to convince even the most well-adjusted adults that they should be spending more time preparing exotic meals for their families, taking their children on extravagant vacations, creating new dance moves with their offspring, and sharing evidence of their parental devotion with the rest of the world.

In this environment, parents are constantly encouraged to invest more time, money, and energy in their children's athletic careers. As their kids advance through the system, many parents find that team camaraderie, even the shared success of playing on a winning team, is insufficient. Beating a rival team or capturing a league championship may produce team accolades, but for many parents the ultimate sign of success is an offer to play for a college team. This individual accomplishment trumps all other honors. Things seem to have shifted from "It's not if you win or lose, it's how you play the game" to "It doesn't matter how your team performs, as long as you get the attention of a college scout." And the more highly ranked the college sports program, the more admirable the accomplishment.

This emphasis on credentials now saturates our culture in many forms and locations. Over the past two decades the two of us have spent a significant amount of time in school classrooms, gymnasiums, and cafeterias. During that period, we noticed a gradual decline in attention paid to students' social development and love for learning. There has been a steady increase in the emphasis placed on product over process. As you probably have experienced yourself, the importance attached to test scores now overshadows many of the core responsibilities our society has traditionally entrusted to schools. As long as students receive high scores on standardized tests, the system is judged a success. One by-product of this shift is that schools may prepare children to win academic competitions—but lose their motivation to learn along the way.

It seems like just about every month a new example of the troubling manifestations of our fixation on results appears in the news. One recent morning, two articles that appeared in *USA Today* caught our attention. One reported on the career of Rick Singer, the man most closely associated with the college admissions bribery scandal that provoked widespread outrage in 2018–19. The second described a brawl that erupted between parents of two Little League teams in Denver. These reports suggest that in schools and in sports, heightened attention to producing results has blurred the lines between appropriate and unacceptable behavior.

Motivated to create opportunities for their children, parents may unconsciously push their children to try harder, aim higher, do more. Settling for less than the ideal can be difficult when adults believe their children's futures are at stake. As Singer's business partner, Joel Margulies, remarked in the *USA Today* piece (by Gregory Korte, 6/24/19), "Everybody has a con. It's just a question of whether you get caught at it."

Notably, Singer's career as an admissions consultant grew out of his work as a high school basketball coach in the 1980s. At the same time he was coaching basketball, Singer founded a company, Future Stars, that purported to help high school student athletes develop a "personal brand" that would help them stand out from other students applying to elite colleges. Before this type of service was commonplace, Singer recognized the earning potential of marketing young athletes. For a fee, Singer created profiles and videos of those athletes, which he sent to college coaches.

Over a period of twenty years, Singer helped hundreds of high school students gain admission to college through "side doors" that included bribing college coaches to recruit his clients as athletes, paying test proctors to cheat on SAT tests, and creating profiles of his clients that superimposed their faces onto photos of other athletes. Eventually, Singer attracted national recognition when he was one of fifty people charged in a college admissions and bribery scam. Under pressure, he pleaded guilty to racketeering conspiracy, money laundering, and obstruction of justice charges.

Clearly, paying someone to take an entrance test for another student or to bribe a coach to endorse an applicant who does not even play sports should not be tolerated. What about activities that may be legal but provide some students with opportunities not offered to other adolescents? Should parents be allowed to help their sons and daughters write college application essays? Should their ability to pay for trips around the world influence decisions made by admissions officers? How about forking over large sums of money to SAT prep coaches?

The second newspaper story we came across reported on a fight that broke out between parents who disagreed with calls made by the home plate umpire at a Little League Baseball game. Things got so heated that approximately twenty adults, male and female, spilled onto the field and started punching each other. Eventually, the police department was forced to respond. To make matters worse, the players were mostly seven-year-olds, and the umpire who made the calls that provoked parental outrage was only thirteen!

This episode highlights the lengths to which parents will go to protect what they believe to be their children's best interests. When their children are not treated as they would like, and sometimes when their children are not performing to their parents' expectations, some parents lose their sense of perspective and behave in uncharacteristic ways. In any other setting, they would probably agree that hurling insults at an umpire or taking part in a physical fight in front of children is unacceptable. On the sidelines of an athletic contest, however, surrounded by other parents eager to see their children succeed, minor events can take on outsized significance. In the heat of the moment, a small number of adults who misbehave can incite enthusiastic, but typically reasonable, parents to overstep the lines of appropriate behavior.

The stories about the college admissions scandal and the Little League brawl underscore the pressures experienced by parents of young athletes. As the youth sports world has expanded and intensified, many parents feel obligated to take a more active role in their children's athletic careers. Rooting your child on is no longer enough. Instead, parents increasingly feel they must constantly advocate for their young athletes, ensuring that their interests are protected.

Negotiating the World of High Stakes Sports

As we conducted our research, we discovered many of the pressures that confronted parents of truly elite athletes have trickled down to lower levels of the youth sports world. Parents are now pressed to make consequential decisions about their children's athletic careers at earlier and earlier points in their lives. Many adults do not initially plan to make athletics such a central component of their children's lives. Quite often, they are encouraged to sign up their elementary school-aged children to play a single sport year-round. As their kids advance through the system, the pressure to go "all in" continues to intensify.

In this environment, maintaining a sense of balance is no easy task. Parents may have the best of intentions for their children but lack the information or broader perspective they need to make wise decisions for their sons and daughters. They frequently lack the time or information to grapple with thorny questions related to their children's social, ethical, and physical development: How much stress should they place on sports? Should they push their children to set ambitious goals for themselves or provide their children with the space to make those decisions for themselves? What sacrifices are worth making if they increase their child's chances of achieving excellence?

There are no simple answers to these questions. They require careful consideration of the individual child, the options available to the young athlete, and the programs available in the community. Yet most parents lack the information necessary to make wise decisions for their kids. Their emotional attachments to their children add an additional layer of tension to the situation. In this environment, decisions that might otherwise seem insignificant can create enormous stress for well-intentioned parents.

Rapid expansion of the youth sports industry has made this situation even more perplexing and stressful for parents. Few have a clear understanding of the full range of options available for their athletic children. Developing an awareness of the ways the youth sports industry operates can help adults make better choices for their children. This book is designed to provide parents with that broad perspective on youth sports—the opportunities it can offer as well as the problematic aspects of competitive sports today.

In this book, we offer insights into the current world of youth sports that draw from the actual experiences of young athletes and their families. Rather than outline a set of steps that parents should follow, we reflect on the forces that influenced the choices made by the families we followed. The experiences shared by those parents add a layer of reality to a topic that is often discussed in extreme terms. We hope this material will help parents make decisions that will help their children to thrive as athletes and as human beings.

CHAPTER ONE

Who's on First?

How Kids' Sports Became Big Business and How It Affects Parents

"I hear complaints from parents. Why aren't you doing this, or why aren't you practicing more frequently, and why aren't you trying to move these kids up to a higher level? Why aren't you doing more, right? And you know some parents are very intense about that, they really see the [local community] program as something that it's not? . . . So, for those parents that say that to me, I would remind them . . . it's about leadership, it's about teaching leadership. It's about teaching being a member of a team, and sacrificing, you know what I mean. All these corny kind of things that you hear, it's true . . . If you want to do more, you want more of an intense experience, you go join the club team and spend $2,000 dollars."

— Parent and local league board member —

A mitt, a ball, and a bat. It wasn't that long ago when that's all you needed to play the game of baseball—along with a bit of competitive spirit. On any given day, a group of kids would spontaneously gather in the playground, as if being called by some greater force, to play ball. The oldest, most confident child was by default captain. A broken window could end the game early, with your buddies running off in every direction. And a game might get rained out occasionally. Otherwise, you could usually count on enough kids showing up for an afternoon of play, friendship, and healthy competition pretty much right outside your front door.

But the days of coming home from school, lacing up your Converse All Stars, grabbing a mitt, and meeting the neighborhood kids for a pick-up baseball game are basically over. Most kids searching for athletic competition no longer play these kinds of games. They play sports. Organized sports. They get outfitted and coached and driven from town to town to increase the competition bandwidth. They play not for a team whose players were cherry picked by the oldest kid on the block but for a commercialized youth sports industry backed by billions of dollars.

Sports have long been embedded in youth culture. Baseball cards, movies, getting your favorite athlete's autograph, tracking player statistics, and talking about last night's game with your friends are commonplace. The sports industry in general seems to have grabbed hold of American culture like no other institution. The grip on society that celebrity athletes and professional sports teams have long held in the United States has gradually seeped into youth sports organizations—affecting not only young players but their parents as well.

Overseeing the athletic activities of young athletes has become more complicated in terms of time, money, and intensity. Kids today have "athletic careers," a sport's season is no longer limited to two or three months, and the pressure on parents to give their child a competitive advantage is at an all-time high.

From 2010 to 2017, the youth sports industry increased by 55 percent and now constitutes a $19 billion market—larger than the NFL! It has rapidly evolved into a complex system with multiple layers and shifting expectations. Over forty million children in the United States play sports today, more than half of all kids between the ages of five and seventeen. And many of them are doing it for more than fun. Before they are eligible to apply for a driver's license, some young athletes are flying across the country to participate in showcase events designed to attract the attention of college scouts. In the middle of all this, and in some ways driving it, are parents, most of whom are utterly confused about what they've gotten themselves and their kids into.

It's Complicated

When our own kids, who were five and six years old at the time, started playing sports in the late 1990s and early 2000s, we were operating on shaky ground. Although both of us played sports when we were younger, our experiences as players were not very helpful to us as parents. While the rules of the games hadn't changed, almost everything else had. It was as if an entirely new industry had sprouted up and replaced the neighborhood-based games and leagues that we associated with youth sports. Unfamiliar with the new youth sports landscape, we relied on our families, advice from other parents, information from local coaches, and lots of trust in adults we barely knew.

We were not alone. We learned in our interviews that other parents were just as lost, sinking into the same sandlot. Very few had a clear sense of what they were signing up for. One mother told us, "I wish someone had told me about this whole structure so we could've more actively made the choice to put our son on a travel team that was on his trajectory and that was his choice."

The structure of youth sports has become increasingly complicated over the years. Many teams are run by independent organizations, each with their own website that highlight various terms, requirements, contracts, levels of play and commitment, skills training, and in some cases the promise of being put on the college athletic scholarship tract.

As these entities are not associated with school systems, they are not part of a school's communication channels. Learning about existing programs requires doing some homework. A Google search will generate a list of leagues and programs available for any given sport by location, but the list can be long with varying price tags and commitment requirements. Wading through the pros and cons of each league can be tiring and time-consuming. And trying to decipher where a child will best fit in is next to impossible.

So while the information may be available to parents eager to seek it out, it is neither easily accessible nor centrally organized. Few of the parents we spoke with took the initiative to conduct this type of research, especially when their children were young.

For parents, following the lead of their friends—many of whom were taking youth sports very seriously—made life easier. Almost no one we spoke to questioned the information they received from other adults in their social circles. This makes sense if we consider that when these parents played organized sports, their options were narrow. In most cases, they signed up for the one softball or basketball league operating in their town. This simplified the lives of athletes as well as their parents. There was no need to think carefully about the consequences of playing for one team over another. The youth sports world was transparent and straightforward.

That is no longer the case. Signing up a child for baseball used to mean showing up for practice and games a few times a week at the neighborhood field. Nowadays, parents and their athletes often must travel an hour from home several times a week for practice and sometimes hundreds of miles every weekend to watch their child play in a league that often may be fun and exciting, for kids and parents, but is built on a foundation of false promises: if you sign up for all these programs and play hard all weeklong, you will excel and go places in the world of sports.

Blindsided by an industry that offers endless opportunities, charges hefty fees, makes tantalizing promises, and has overtaken some of the simpler avenues for youth sports, many parents feel overwhelmed. Importantly, most parents don't fully understand what they are getting their children—and themselves—into.

What Youth Sports Means for Families Today

The commercialization of youth sports has its pros, some of which we'll address later in this chapter and elsewhere in the book. But the complex structure that has evolved in response to this commercialization is adversely affecting many parents today, especially since the rules seem to change mid-game.

For instance, two of the parents we interviewed, Helen and Nathan Peterson, enjoy sports, but athletics has never been the center of their lives. When their son, Jason, expressed an interest in soccer, they encouraged him to pursue that interest without giving it a lot of thought. Starting when he was four, Jason participated in an after-school program at the local Y. When he aged out of that program, he joined a team for first and second graders that practiced near the Petersons' home. Although the team played games every Saturday, no one kept score and parents took turns serving as referees.

All the kids in the neighborhood who were interested in soccer joined this league. It was fun, and there weren't really any alternatives.

In the fall of second grade, Jason started to feel bored by the town league. He no longer found it challenging. But by the time Jason realized he wanted something more, none of the travel teams in his town were accepting new players that season. The Petersons started talking to parents of Jason's classmates and learned that one of his closest friends was playing for a team in a neighboring town. So they signed up Jason to try out for that team. When he was offered a spot on the club, the Petersons accepted, without giving the idea much thought.

Things immediately changed for Jason—and his family. They quickly learned that "with travel soccer, you're all in." The shift from a casual team to a more involved travel league was disruptive, especially since it involved more time and transportation. When asked to clarify, Nathan explained, "It rules your life. It means you're going to practice twice a week; you're going to games at least once a week. We heard that some parents also practiced with their kids to improve their skills and that type of thing, but we didn't do that."

Jason enjoyed being part of the team and traveling to tournaments in other cities, hanging out in the hotel with his teammates, and swimming in the hotel pool. And his soccer skills improved noticeably, but so did the pressure.

Helen recalled that "the team went from being a team where they'd travel from just the surrounding towns to I don't know how these levels work. It's very complicated. They kept moving up. And the coach would just tell us, 'Oh, now we're part of this new league, we're part of a premier league.'" At the time, the Petersons didn't even know what a premier league was.

Although Jason's parents hadn't anticipated this rapid escalation in demands, they didn't object. As Nathan related, "We knew a travel team involved playing against other towns, but the whole progression wasn't really clear to us." They also discovered that kids were required to try out for the team every year and not everyone made the cut. "There was a little bit of pressure of, well, I might not even be able to continue on the team I'm already on." To the Petersons, this system seemed very political.

Rather than explore other options, the Petersons went with the flow. According to Helen, "The travel kept getting ratcheted up and the number of tournaments they wanted to play ratcheted up." Some weekends the team played games in another part of the state, which could eat up an entire day.

By the time Jason entered eighth grade, his interest in soccer began to fade. By that point, Helen lamented, "It was all about winning, always winning. And getting yelled at by this team captain. Little by little, it was getting rougher. It was getting more competitive." At the end of the season, Jason decided he had had enough and left the team. This created the space for him to participate in activities he had previously been interested in, but never had enough time for—playing a musical instrument, Model UN, mountain biking, and running on the school track team.

Looking back at their son's experiences, the Petersons acknowledge the advantages of playing travel soccer. For example, Jason made some good friends and saw the benefits of committing to a challenging task. According to Helen, "He also learned a lot about people—dealing with aggressive people. I think it's made him a lot less afraid."

Knowing what they know now, would they have signed Jason up for a different team? "Maybe, yeah," admitted Nathan, "because that was not our agenda at all." Helen concurred, "Yes, but I don't even know how one would go about figuring that out when your kid is only eight. It was confusing. I didn't know how things worked. I didn't know that he could have signed up for teams in other towns or which travel team played at level two and which team played at level three. He only signed up for the Pumas because his friend was on it."

This approach to decision-making does provide some tangible benefits. For example, adjusting to a new team may be easier when a child already knows people on the team and parents can more easily find other adults to drive their kids to practices and games. However, as the Petersons' story illustrates, choosing a team entirely based on word of mouth may have long-term consequences that they did not initially consider. The time and money demanded of players, for instance, often increases exponentially.

In previous generations, kids typically switched teams after the conclusion of each (short) season. But today, kids like Jason may play for the same team year-round for several years. This can make it difficult to step back, think about how things are going with their current team, and consider alternatives. Players and their families tend to make commitments that turn out to be long-term while they are still in the second or third grade.

While competitive sports may affect the young athlete most directly, significant demands are placed on all family members. During the first year or two, those demands may be restricted to duties such as volunteering in the concession stand a couple of times or supplying refreshments at games. But things can quickly escalate, requiring parents to devote entire weekends to chaperoning their children and driving them to other states.

The commitment and the price tag almost always turn out to be substantial—and not just for elite athletes. Kids as young as six or seven are being swept up in the flurry, giving up (or never signing up for) other activities they might also enjoy so they can specialize in one sport. On the other end of the spectrum, many preteens avoid sports altogether in the face of the commitment expected of them.

The Petersons' experience is typical and underscores the opacity of the youth sports world today. Parents try to do what's best for their children but may not understand how to do that. Confronted by a system that looks very different from what they experienced as kids, they make decisions on the fly by following the lead of their friends.

When—and how—did youth sports become so big, serious, complicated, and expensive? One way to find out is to follow recent trends.

From Little League to Elite Academy

Reports that document the number of children who regularly participate in sports provide a rather confusing portrait of the field by offering some general information about the popularity of sports. For example, a report published by the National Federation of State High School Associations (NFHS), the organization that writes the rules of competition for most high school sports, indicates that there has been a steady increase in the number of students who play on high school teams. Rates of participation doubled between 1971–72 and 2023–24, growing from 3,960,932 to 8,062,302.[1]

Broad demographic trends, however, fail to capture some critical changes in the structure of the youth sports world. Overall numbers of participants may have changed only slightly in recent years, but the types of sports children play have shifted in some pretty remarkable ways. These modifications are affecting participants as well as their families. They have redefined our understanding of concepts such as "season," "team," and "success."

Only a few years ago, kids had few options when it came to sports. They signed up for a local AYSO soccer team or Pop Warner football team in the fall, shifted to a YMCA or church-affiliated basketball team in the winter, and when the weather got better moved back outdoors, joining a neighborhood swim team or recreational baseball or softball league for a few months. When they entered middle or high school, students who wished to continue playing sports typically tried out for their school teams. For the vast majority of young athletes, sports were community-based and cyclical. Playing sports was something they participated in with other kids in the neighborhood for short spurts of time.

Options available to young athletes may have been limited, but this created flexibility for students and parents. Teenagers with multiple interests could participate in a variety of extracurricular activities. During a single school year, for instance, a motivated student could compete for the varsity swim team, act in a school play, and play on a Babe Ruth baseball club. Only the exceptionally talented were recruited to play a sport year-round or for an out-of-town team. And because most activities were community-based, the demands placed on parents were minimal.

Over the past decade or so, these patterns have shifted markedly. The assumptions that once guided parents as they made decisions about their children's extracurricular activities have been upended. For instance, signing up your child for a community-based team is no longer possible in some locations. Many local sports leagues are no longer supported, having been edged out by the steady growth of the youth sports industry. According to Kirsten Hextrum, a professor at the University of Oklahoma, "Over the course of the past, say, thirty years, we've had a defunding of sports within our community and school systems. But a parallel occurrence has happened alongside that, which is: We've had an increase of private sports clubs popping up to replace what was once done by low-cost, recreational or school sports."[2]

This decline in community-based programs happened swiftly. For example, in 2010, one town league in the area where we conducted our research had enough players to field six baseball teams composed of town residents. Just ten years later, the same town merged with another to form a single team that played against teams in other towns, forcing parents to drive farther than anticipated for a "community-based" league. This trend is happening in towns big and small across the country. For example, participation in Little League Baseball declined by 1–3 percent annually over the past twenty years or so.[3]

The Birth of the Travel Team—For Everyone

In the youth sports world of today, community-based programs are no longer considered adequate—even for an "average" athlete. On the other hand, people view travel teams as more prestigious and rigorous. Parents and kids have been swept up in a campaign that tells an intriguing narrative: Sports is about being the best you can be, so why not play for a team that will bring out your best? Families began buying into the idea that the type of team their child played for during their elementary school years would determine their athletic opportunities in high school, college, and perhaps even in the professional ranks. And the kids, in turn, would have a better experience. Once this collective mindset took over, the popularity of travel teams exploded.

In the not-too-distant past, playing on a travel club that competed against teams from other towns in the area would have been relatively rare, available only for the most dedicated young athletes. Over the past decade, however, travel teams have been organized for almost every sport that might interest a child, from soccer to basketball to lacrosse. Travel sports teams have gained cache among young athletes and their parents. Playing for an elite academy or regional team has become the new marker of status for the competitive athlete. In response to this increased demand for spots on travel clubs, the industry continues to expand, becoming more hierarchical, expensive, time-consuming, and regionally expansive. The race to the top, it sometimes seems, has no end point.

In the area where we conducted our research, interest in travel sports has led to the emergence of new leagues, clubs, and teams to meet the increased demand for more serious athletics. One town (with a population of fewer than 30,000 residents) organizes four boys travel soccer teams at each age level! The total number of travel teams is so great that for some sports, teams are grouped into four or five divisions. Further complicating this picture are regional teams, sports academies, and Olympic Development Programs, which operate parallel to more traditional travel programs.

One result of the rapid growth of the industry is that almost any motivated athlete can obtain a spot on a travel team. She may not earn a spot on a top-tier travel team, but if she tries out for multiple clubs, she will probably receive an offer from a team located lower on the competitive hierarchy, which may require a drive of an hour or more to regular training sessions. This increased access has created new opportunities. Children who in the past might have had limited options beyond the local youth sports program can now play for clubs that compete against teams from other cities and towns and across state lines. They can also learn from experienced, often paid, coaches rather than parents who lacked deep knowledge of a sport.

What's driving the change? How do we explain these shifts in the world of youth sports? Why would parents choose to spend more time and money, and why would kids give up playing other sports, joining the theater club, or having free time with friends on weekends all for the sake of one sport?

It would be misleading to present a clear and definite explanation for the changes that have taken place in youth sports. A multitude of influences have combined to shift perceptions about the purposes of youth sports and to impel changes in behavior. To more fully understand why the youth sports industry has become the entity that it is, we need to follow the money—and the dreams. As we analyzed the decisions made by the parents, coaches, and athletes we studied, two factors seemed particularly salient: the dream of landing a spot on a college team and the sheer number of programs available to aid in this process.

Pipe Dreams and Prestige

There is a pipeline that connects high school and college athletics. In previous generations, an adolescent athlete could attract the attention of college recruiters by excelling in high school contests. Individuals who earned all-league honors or set individual records were likely to appear on the radar of college coaches. The more prestigious the awards garnered, the higher level of interest an athlete was likely to receive. Although elite regional teams did operate, they were comparatively small in number. Playing for a team that competed regionally was reserved for truly exceptional athletes, not a prerequisite for making the transition from high school to college sports.

As parents began to find ways to make their sons and daughters stand out from the crowd, simply playing for a high school team was no longer considered sufficient—no matter how talented a young player might have appeared. This mindset impelled a steady increase in families who decided that community-based sports was not enough for their children. Parents eager to create advantages for their children signed them up for more competitive clubs. These organizations ranged from teams composed of talented athletes living in a particular town who were brought together to compete against clubs from neighboring cities to "academies" sponsored by professional teams.

The costs, frequency of practices, and goals for players on these types of teams varied significantly. Some were branches of recreational leagues, while others were profit-making operations that charged exorbitant fees (often referred to as "pay-to-play" programs). The structure of this sprawl of teams may have been difficult to understand, but one thing was clear—if players (or their parents) decided their current team was not delivering what they needed, they could always try to climb the ladder to a more intense or elite club.

The principles of supply and demand began to rule the growing youth sports market. Besides having the option to try out for multiple levels of teams, they could also pay for individual coaching, training, and marketing assistance. When a particular organization or service became saturated, a more elite—and often more expensive—form of that entity materialized. For example, single-day coaching clinics were supplemented by multiple-session or even year-round training courses. Businesses with names such as "The Baseball Training Institute," "Bases Loaded," "Extra Innings," and "Strikeforce Baseball" emerged to cater to the needs of ambitious baseball players. The method to the madness worked. Today, we could compile lists like this for virtually any sport.

This colossal, constantly expanding youth sports marketplace communicated to parents that if their child was to have a realistic chance of playing at the college level, investing in supplemental services would be necessary. Whether this perception is accurate does not really matter. Once the "keeping up with the Joneses" mentality became widespread, it took on a life of its own. Many parents believed their children might be at a disadvantage if they did not play for an elite club, attend year-round conditioning classes, or purchase expensive equipment. Saying no to potential opportunities would be like intentionally holding back their kids. So they began writing checks.

As the number of youth sports consumers increased, so did the quantity of athletes who began chasing the dream of a college sports career. Students who wanted to play college basketball signed up for everything basketball. They gave their chosen sport their undivided time and attention. The days of cross-training were coming to a close. No longer were kids playing football, baseball, and hockey over the course of a year. Sports specialization became commonplace.

In this context, travel teams started to make sense. Why pass your time playing Little League, which anyone can do, if it is possible to gain a spot on a team that has sent players to the University of Arizona? Does it make sense to spend weekends competing against other kids from the neighborhood if you could spend that time playing in a tournament attended by college scouts? The number of slots on NCAA teams remained constant, yet the percentage of adolescents who partake in some activity billed as increasing one's chances of attracting the attention of a college coach continued to grow, a subject we cover in-depth in Chapter Four.

The Principles of Supply and Demand

The second factor feeding the expansion of the youth sports industry is the economic drive of people alert to the income-generating potential of supplemental services. The youth sports market seems to feed itself. An army of entrepreneurs offers its services to parents motivated to make their kids stand out from the incessantly expanding crowd of serious athletes. These businesspeople range from former athletes who offer private lessons in their garages to multimillion dollar corporations that organize dozens of "pay-to-play" teams. Both the number of young athletes who think they have a chance at playing sports in college and the adults with novel schemes for increasing the odds of that happening seem limitless.

The most visible layer of the youth sports industry consists of individual coaches, trainers, and team managers. Mothers and fathers continue to devote their free time to coaching community-based teams, but they are usually viewed as inferior to coaches who charge for their services. The more impressive the coach's resume, the more exorbitant the fees they can charge. Playing for a team helmed by a college coach or a former professional athlete can be especially pricey. To justify these fees, elite coaches promise young athletes superior skill development as well as access to college recruiters.

Playing for a well-regarded coach, though, is often not considered enough. Ambitious athletes are signing up for private coaching or training sessions in greater numbers. In close proximity to where we conducted our research, young athletes can sign up for almost any type of sports-related personal service. Here are a few possibilities:

- Basketball Training Academy (Cost: $100 for six-week training session)
    + Staff works with players on basic basketball skills, fundamentals, coordination, and agility in small groups
    + Grades K–8
    + Focus is on skill development with no games played

- Scholar-Athlete Assessment (Cost: $350)
    + One-hour meeting with player and their parents
    + Baseball skills evaluation
    + Academic evaluation
    + Review of questionnaire, including list of target colleges
    + Honest evaluation of the student-athlete's prospects of playing at the college level

- Strength and Conditioning Program (Cost: $360 for twelve sessions)
    + Small training groups
    + Programs that help to maximize each athlete's gains in overall athletic performance

- Catchers Glovework Program (Cost: $1,050 for ten weeks)
    + One hour of strength training, two times per week
    + One hour of glovework training, two times per week
    + Open gym hours
    + Total of fifty hours of training

- Gymnastics Academy
    + Private lesson (Cost: $65 per hour)
    + Group training clinic ($15 per child per hour; minimum six people)
    + USAG competitive team ($65–$700 per month, depending on level)

Online counseling services is another segment of the youth sports industry that has expanded rapidly in recent years. The pressure to excel on the field and reach maximum physical potential is now coupled with an entirely different skill set: Kids also need to market themselves to college recruiters.

Athletes who play for elite teams are likely to become the targets of businesses that offer to help with every aspect of the recruiting process. The home page for CaptainU, for instance, proclaims that "More than two million athletes have used CaptainU Athlete to follow their dreams of making a great college team. Put your best foot forward, never get stuck, and move with confidence." Using CaptainU, kids can "Build a recruiting resume that stands out with stats, pictures, videos, and evals from your coaches and friends." Although the site offers a basic package for free, upgrading to plans that offer more extensive services that range in cost from $19.95/month to $199.95/month. Customers can create a "cutting edge recruiting profile," upload videos of themselves in action to their CaptainU web page, search for information about colleges, send letters of interest directly to college coaches, and receive information about recruiting camps. CaptainU is one of many companies that provides online support to young athletes. In the area we conducted our research, young athletes often created profiles on websites like CaptainU around the time they entered high school and sent them to college coaches. It was not clear if recruiters looked closely at those profiles but that didn't deter athletes. Rather, they seemed motivated by the logic of "if I don't do it, I might be at a disadvantage."

The Cost of Success

The costs associated with playing on a Little League team or a local soccer team tend to be straightforward; registration fees cover uniforms, coaching, referees, and so forth. Families may need to set aside some additional funds for snacks or equipment, but those costs are usually manageable. Playing at the elite level is a whole different ballgame. In addition to higher monthly fees, parents are usually expected to pay for travel to other cities or states, specialized equipment, and tournament entry fees, not to mention "optional" activities and services to enhance skill sets.

The costs of climbing the youth sports ladder can be exorbitant. According to a report published in *TIME* magazine, the youth sports industry increased by 55 percent between 2010 and 2017.[4] According to one research organization, the US youth sports market generated a total of $19.2 billion in revenue in 2019 and was projected to skyrocket to $77.5 billion by the year 2026.[5] For families, the cumulative costs of playing for a travel team vary significantly but typically total between $1,500 and $3,000 per year, per child.[6] In many cases, families will spend as much as 10.5 percent of their household income on the expenses associated with youth sports.[7]

○   ○   ○

The youth sports world has become more convoluted, hierarchical, and intense over the past twenty years. Institutions that were once thought of as cultural anchors are quickly becoming obsolete. Neighborhood-based leagues are having trouble competing with elite teams that nurture the ambitions of young athletes and their parents. Participants seem to have shifted their gaze upward, focusing on the next level of competition or the more prestigious college showcase. This recalibration of what it means to be a successful athlete has led people at all levels of the system to modify their behavior. And the system appears to be constantly metastasizing in response to the growing demand for specialized services.

The rapid expansion of the youth sports industry and the challenges this has created for families raises many tough questions. One question of particular importance is: What happens to the young athletes whose families lack the resources to compete in this marketplace and who must rely solely on their physical and mental talents? In Chapter Two, we explore that question, and share the stories of families who tried to answer it.

CHAPTER TWO

Why They Do It?

....

"When we grew up, we didn't have travel teams: twelve
game seasons, playoffs, All Stars, that was it. I would
have loved it. So, to have them have that opportunity,
and they love baseball. It's something they love doing,
so I'd rather have them keep busy doing it."

— *Parent of travel baseball players* —

....

Parents have been signing up their kids for sports for decades. Playing on a team is viewed as an essential feature of childhood, like participating in scouts or going to camp. It seems as though many people play on a Little League softball or baseball team in elementary school, regardless of their athletic prowess. The assumption that kids will participate in sports is so widespread that we tend not to invest a lot of thought about why parents should or should not encourage their children to play on a sports team. It's just something we do. Not signing up your child to play on a team might even raise questions about your priorities.

But the decision to sign up a child to play on a particular team can have long-lasting consequences. That is especially true today, given the expansion of the youth sports industry described in the previous chapter. Until fairly recently, sports were generally viewed as one of numerous activities that attracted the attention of children at some point during the year. An elementary school student might practice gymnastics once or twice a week, take piano lessons another day, and spend the rest of the week playing with her friends. That is no longer the norm. Children's lives have become more structured, plotted, and intense. According to the National PTA, "kids playing after school is becoming a thing of the past."[8] Extracurricular activities that were previously considered inconsequential are now regarded as critical features of an individual's social and emotional development. Parents often feel compelled to fill up their children's free time with structured activities from the time they start school.

Given this shift toward more strategic management of children's social lives, it makes sense to carefully consider how parents make decisions about which athletic activities to sign up their children for. In this chapter, we tackle this topic, highlighting the factors that tend to exert the strongest influence over adults as they oversee their children's athletic activities. As we note, when their children are young, parents often approach extracurricular activities with a sense of altruistic optimism. Shaped by their own memories of childhood, they assume any opportunities to participate in sports will serve their sons and daughters well.

Adults' attitudes toward athletics, however, can rapidly shift. As a result of recent intensification within the youth sports industry, parents may feel pressure to take a more strategic approach to overseeing their children's extracurricular activities than was necessary when they were growing up. For a variety of reasons, many parents today search for activities that will keep their children busy—and give them advantages over other children. How they respond to that pressure can be quite revealing. Our interviews with parents underscore how difficult it is to maintain a sense of perspective within a system that treats sports as business and encourages athletes to specialize before they enter adolescence.

In this chapter, we also explore the factors that shape the decisions made by parents of young athletes, the way their thinking changes over time, and the consequences of the choices they make. The ideas parents shared with us indicate that media accounts of sports parents may reinforce stereotypes that don't accurately capture their experiences. Many adults are just a couple of steps ahead of their children as they manage their athletic careers. Operating in an environment that has undergone such dramatic shifts since they were in school, parents constantly move forward, not always sure they are making the right choices.

Early Motivations

Up to this point in the book, we have emphasized changes in youth sports that have taken place over the past two decades. At early levels of the system, however, things have remained fairly constant. As was true in previous generations, parents sign up their children to play sports for a variety of reasons, with the best of intentions. Most of the parents we interviewed enrolled their sons and daughters in t-ball leagues or introductory basketball clinics with the goal of providing them opportunities to play, get some exercise, and make friends. Few of these people had developed long-term plans for their children. Lacking reliable information about the full range of options available to their kids, they tended to follow the lead of other families in their communities.

Initially, expectations and pressures remained, for the most part, low. Athletic leagues for young children are often organized to minimize competition among players—and parents. In t-ball games, for example, every player receives an equal number of at-bats and scores are not kept; in soccer leagues, teams are prohibited from running up the score. The emphasis is on teamwork, skill development, and sportsmanship. Parents can enjoy the experience of watching their children participate in sports without looking very far into the future.

This period of playing for enjoyment, though, is fleeting. As a result of the expansion and commercialization of the youth sports industry documented in Chapter One, parents today are likely to be encouraged to consider alternatives to community-based leagues for their children a year or two after they begin playing organized sports. In some cases, the motivation to search for "better" options is internal; when their children display athletic talent, parents start to think about how to harness those talents. In other cases, external forces encourage parents to take their sons' and daughters' athletic careers more seriously. Friends, coaches, or private enterprises may nudge them to sign up for more competitive leagues or training services.

When we asked parents why they had moved their children from town-based leagues to travel teams, they offered a wide range of reasons. The most common explanations for making the change related to perceived shortcomings of community-based leagues. One parent told us, for instance, that Little League Baseball and Softball is "a dying breed." This dissatisfaction related to the quality of coaching as well as the level of play. According to another parent, in the town league, there was "not a lot of discipline. Kids aren't really serious, you know. Really just goofing off, doing stupid things, and not coming to practice, and then parents yelling at the coach about playing when they don't come to practice."

For parents disappointed with the quality of local leagues in their towns, travel sports may constitute an appealing alternative. Twenty years ago, spots on travel teams were reserved for exceptional athletes. The exclusive nature of these elite clubs provided some protection for community-based leagues. Because so few athletes played travel sports, less competitive leagues could depend on a steady supply of players. That is no longer the case. In towns around the country, the exodus of young athletes from community-based leagues to travel teams has upended the status quo. For large numbers of players and their families, local organizations like Little League are viewed as a less attractive alternative to programs that sponsor year-round play and compete against teams from other cities. Community-based leagues have become stepping stones to bigger things.

Repercussions of Moving Up

After making the switch from community-based to travel teams, parents usually find themselves spending more hours shuttling their children to practices, attending games, and volunteering in the snack booth. This escalation in commitment tends to spur a related expansion in the psychological attention parents devote to athletics. Joining a travel team often triggers a recalibration of action and attitude for everyone involved. Playing sports quickly changes from one of many extracurricular activities that occupy the time of children to *the* central focus. Few of the parents we interviewed were fully prepared for this change. As one mother reflected, "I wish someone had told me about this whole structure so we could have more actively made the choice to put him on a travel team that was on this trajectory . . . We're not against the trajectory, but I think there were more options." While these parents didn't have regrets, they recognized, in retrospect, that the family commitment to a travel team, including regular weekend trips, wasn't something they had anticipated or carefully planned for.

In one sense, this tendency to invest more time and energy in a child's sports activities as they get older is not surprising. For generations, children have become more focused about their extracurricular activities as they mature. It seems logical for a person interested in playing a musical instrument or dancing to spend more time practicing those activities in high school than they did in elementary school. What has changed, though, is that expansion of the youth sports industry is driving families to commit to year-round sports at much earlier points in the careers of young athletes. Most of the players we followed joined their first travel team when they were nine- or ten-years-old.

Another significant change is that as travel sports have become more ubiquitous, and as the status of community-based sports has declined, pressure to sign up a child for a team that plays year-round has also become more potent. Parents may be bombarded by messages from a variety of sources—their children, other parents, coaches, trainers—all encouraging them to make the switch to travel sports. These might range from direct pleas from sons or daughters who want to join the travel team their friends play on to intangible worries that they should be doing more for their kids. Under these conditions, resisting the pressure to join a travel team could be regarded as risky. Many adults worry that if their child doesn't commit to play on a club team while in elementary school, they might never have that chance again.

Once they decided to move their child from community-based to travel sports programs, though, the parents we spoke with usually expressed satisfaction with that decision. Despite the increased demands that were placed on them, most adults indicated that their efforts were rewarded. When asked what advice she would give to a parent thinking about signing up a child to play travel sports, one mother responded, "Sit back and enjoy it. The thought of doing it is scarier than actually doing it. When you start out, you may not realize what you're getting into, but it all works out, especially if you get along with the other families on the team." Another volunteered, "If your child is happy, if you're not forcing them to do something they don't want to do, they will have a positive experience." A third parent commented, "I think there's a lot of benefits they can get out of it. It's very time-consuming, and you need to be prepared for that—for the time commitment, the financial commitment—so they really need to be prepared for that. But I think the benefits really outweigh some of that stuff. I do."

Perceived Benefits of Travel Sports

What specific benefits did parents believe justified the demands placed on their families? In reflecting on the positive facets of travel sports, parents highlighted a range of benefits. Those benefits fell into three broad categories: athletic, social, and psychological.

Athletic

The topic that elicited the most attention from parents was level of play. All of the people we interviewed felt that since switching from community-based to travel clubs, their children had been pushed to play at higher levels. A number of influences combined to produce these improvements: players who were motivated to work hard, experienced coaches, year-round training, and challenging competition. Among parents, there was a clear consensus that their children had become better athletes as a result of joining a travel team.

Parents often appreciated the dedication that was demanded of all participants in travel sports. This seriousness about sports was seen as a positive alternative to local leagues that emphasized the value of participating in sports rather than winning. As the father of one soccer player commented, "The style with the [travel team] is much more intense. It's two degrees more intense than the team she was on. When she was on the other team, that was not required of her and it bothered the heck out of me. So I told her she almost had a two-year vacation from working hard." Another parent related that he decided to move his son to travel soccer team so that he could "play on a competitive team because he was ready. Half the time, they didn't even have a full team show up [on the town team]. The next step, if you're serious, is to keep moving, taking the next step. So this was the next step for him." Like many of the adults we spoke with, these parents believed that if their children did not make the transition to travel sports, they would be missing out on critical opportunities to improve their skills.

Most mothers and fathers we interviewed valued the increased level of seriousness displayed by travel team players and coaches. The parent of a baseball player, for example, told us that on a travel team "you're with a group of kids that all want to be there. They're in line with you in terms of wanting to win the game, serious about winning the game." This pervasive devotion to winning placed more pressure on children—but also challenged them to develop as athletes. In contrast with recreational leagues, which many parents felt coddled players, travel teams set high expectations and helped young athletes meet those standards. In other words, they believed the extensive demands placed on players were justified. Parents sometimes expressed concerns about coaches who took winning more seriously than they would have liked but were generally pleased with the mentoring their children received. Extreme behavior was treated as an unavoidable by-product of competitive play.

Not only did most of the parents we interviewed indicate that participating in travel sports was essential to their children's athletic development, but they also tended to frame the transition as a natural, almost unavoidable, development. "The town teams just weren't competitive," one father explained to us, "and she was just kind of plowing through everybody and scoring all of the goals. So we needed to give her more competition." "It was just kind of a natural progression," another parent explained to us. "It grew out of the recreational programs that he was doing. You got this core group of the most dedicated parents and most talented kids and then they want to do more than what's available through the regular rec program." From this perspective, parents are simply responding to their children's evolving needs. "He wanted to play travel at an earlier age and I held him back," one mother told us. "But I finally let him play. I wasn't ready for travel but he was." As this comment suggests, many parents believe that not signing up their children to play travel sports would be doing them a disservice.

Social

Another benefit of travel sports that interviewees highlighted concerned the social connections their children formed with other players. Although players who participate in community-based sports also make friends, the nature of those relationships tends to be more fleeting due to the shorter seasons and regular reforming of teams. Individuals who decide to join travel teams, in contrast, often play for those clubs for several years. In addition, the number of hours they spend interacting with teammates in a given week can be significant. On top of the regular weekly practices they attend, players frequently participate in multiple-day tournaments held in other cities and states. As one parent observed, "Hey, with travel soccer you're all in. . . . It rules your life." One positive outcome of the heavy demands placed on players and their families was expanded opportunities to forge close bonds with other participants over time.

Even adults who expressed concerns about the amount of time their sons and daughters devoted to travel sports appreciated the relationships their children formed with other players. When asked about the most positive aspects of her children's experiences with sports, one mother responded, "The team aspect. I mean, her teammates are her best friends, so I like that social part of it."

Parents valued the support their children received from other players, on and off the field. They provided numerous examples of specific ways that relationships with other players made their sons and daughters feel valued and capable. For example, the father of a high school baseball player explained that when his family moved to the area from another city, his son initially had trouble making new friends. His teammates were the ones who helped him adjust to his new surroundings. Another father contrasted his daughter's soccer friends with her school friends, concluding that "I think the biggest differentiator, or what's unique about her connection with the soccer players, is that they're more driven. They're better at time management. They're better at staying focused." In contrast to his daughter's soccer teammates, this father noted that his daughter had "no connection, nothing in common" with classmates from elementary school. Some interviewees even referred to players and parents as members of their soccer or sports "families."

In an era when some adolescents spend the bulk of their time in front of screens, these parents were grateful their sons and daughters cultivated such close relationships with other children in real time. "I have been thinking about how so many kids just go home after school and play video games all day," one father told us, and how sad that is and how they don't realize all the other things they could be doing." Through travel sports, in contrast, his son constantly interacted with a group of motivated kids who supported one another and formed a social safety net for his son.

Psychological

A related category of benefits parents frequently highlighted encompassed the intangible lessons their children learned through sports. These included things like persistence, the ability to work with others, self-confidence, time management, and resilience. Though children could acquire these skills through a variety of activities, parents felt the intensity of travel sports created challenges that forced their children to adapt in unique ways. In their view, competitive athletics created conditions that mirrored the realities of the real world their children would eventually enter. As one mother posited, "They're always trying to improve themselves, and I think in life, she will carry those skills over."

Several parents observed that the emphasis on participation rather than winning that they experienced in community-based sports undercut the cultivation of life lessons. When "everyone gets a trophy," to use a common cliché, participants may not feel compelled to dig deep and overcome obstacles. One father put it, "These kids—and I'm not just talking about athletically talented ones—we make them think you're always going to win at whatever you do. You are going to get a trophy. You are going to get congratulated. As you get older, you find out that's not the way it works. It's a meritocracy. I don't know, maybe young athletes learn that lesson sooner than the rest of their peers." From this perspective, travel sports present formative challenges that are not likely to surface through more relaxed athletic leagues.

Media accounts often highlight the disturbing effects of excessive competition in youth sports today. While the parents we interviewed did criticize players and coaches who behaved inappropriately, they tended to express appreciation for the challenges that flow from serious competition. According to one father, "The sense of commitment, committing to something and sticking with it even when it's tough, is a lesson every kid should learn." Being thrust into stressful situations, another parent told us, "puts you in situations that you're not going to have academically. Everything's on the line in this moment and you're standing on the mound. Being the pitcher in this situation is one of the toughest things you're going to do anywhere in your life, right? You've got to throw one more strike, right? This is great character-building stuff, you know."

The mother of a soccer player related that in middle school her son "had a little issue with his behavior and his grades." Teachers told her that her son's inability to focus was creating problems for the boy, who was not motivated to apply himself in school. Soccer, on the other hand, required him to concentrate for extended periods of time—and interested him. The parent emphasized to her son that if he didn't get good grades, he wouldn't be able to play soccer. This motivated the boy to try harder in school, and his grades improved. In this way, the parents encouraged their son to apply the focus he displayed on the soccer field to his studies, with positive results.

Shifting Priorities

One important aspect of this issue is parents' views about sports are not static; they evolve over time. The goals that influenced the decisions made by parents often shifted in response to the demands placed on their children, the information they had access to, and the social circles that organized their lives. When the stakes of the game increased, some families chose to withdraw from travel sports. This most often occurred when players were in the eighth or ninth grade. For those who continued to participate in travel sports, though, the stakes of the game steadily increased. The travel team often became the center of their social lives— for children as well as their parents (see Chapter Three for more information about parent communities).

As children advanced through the hierarchy of youth sports, most parents continued to value the positive outcomes discussed above (athletic development, social connections, and life lessons). Things often became complicated, though, due to the growing presence of an additional influence: the possibility of earning an offer, or even a scholarship, to play sports in college. At first glance, parents of young athletes seemed to fall into two camps: those who hoped their investments in travel sports would pay off in the form of an offer from a college coach, and those who insisted they did not want their children to continue playing organized sports after they graduated from high school. Our analysis of interviews with parents suggests the distinction was not that clear cut. When they addressed the topic of collegiate athletics, most parents expressed uncertainty, confusion, and contradictory feelings.

Some interviewees stated without reservation or apology that they hoped their sons or daughters would continue to play sports in the NCAA. "It's a sport she wants to play in college," one mother told us, "so [playing on a travel team] is preparing her, hopefully, for many scholarships." This is not surprising, given the large investments parents invested in their children's athletic careers. By the time they entered high school, these players were playing a sport for most of the year, traveling throughout the region to participate in tournaments, and playing in showcase events attended by college scouts. Many also signed up for recruiting camps held on university campuses, enrolled in supplemental training and coaching clinics, opened accounts with companies that promoted young athletes, and put together highlights videos they could send to NCAA coaches. A few of the athletes we followed missed travel team activities to attend national showcase events held in other parts of the country. For families of such individuals, the ultimate goal of playing sports was clear.

Other parents stated unequivocally that they did not want their children to play sports in college. These individuals expressed concerns about the extensive demands placed on collegiate athletes and the possible negative impact that such a commitment might have on academics. "I would have nothing against her playing club ball in college, but I don't want that to be her focus," one mother told us. "There are so many parents who will do whatever it takes to get them an offer. I'm on the other side." Adults with this view tended to emphasize the social benefits and life skills their children acquired through sports. The father of a soccer player, for example, related that "I've never told her this, but my wish is for her not to play in college. I have nothing against her playing club ball in college, but I don't want it to be her focus. A lot of parents have this idea that their daughter's going to play Division I soccer and because I don't have that illusion, maybe I'm more laid back about it."

A majority of the parents we spoke with, however, seemed unsure or conflicted about their children's futures. Many of these parents initially signed up their children to play travel sports without thinking carefully about the consequences. The choices they made were based on the immediate needs or interests of their children rather than carefully plotted long-term plans. As their sons and daughters advanced through the youth sports hierarchy, though, it became more difficult to resist the temptation to dream about college sports opportunities. It appeared that these parents, even after being involved in travel sports for several years, were still trying to figure out the ultimate goals of those experiences. Often, they emphasized the importance of social development over winning and downplayed their ambitions for their children—but also made comments that indicated they hoped their sons and daughters would receive offers to play sports in college. Some contradicted themselves, without realizing they were doing so. The following juxtaposition of comments made by three mothers in a group interview illustrates this type of internal conflict:

Q: Do you think your son will play soccer in college?	Q: How would you feel if your son decided to quit soccer?
P1: It's up to him.	**P1:** I think I'd cry. Really. That would be hard.
P2: I think he wants to.	**P2:** I can't even fathom that.
P3: I think he wants to. I'll support him either way.	**P3:** If he didn't play in college, I would be sad, but I'd understand.

Like many of the people we interviewed, these parents conveyed mixed messages about the reasons their children were playing sports. After years of involvement in travel sports, they had yet to develop a clear or coherent vision of what those experiences were leading toward.

The three mothers cited above understood at some level that they should not attach too much importance to the college recruitment process. Fully buying into that system might ultimately set up their children for failure. It could also force them to draw connections between themselves and the over-the-top sports parents on other teams who they found repugnant. Yet they also could not completely resist the temptation to dream large. In this precarious situation, adopting an attitude of "I don't expect my child to play sports in college, but if it happens, that would be great" provided them with some psychological insurance. On the surface, they wanted little more than for their children to derive pleasure from sports. The reality was much more complicated.

Searching for Clarity

The mothers and fathers we interviewed expressed a multitude of thoughts about the benefits of taking sports seriously. Some talked at length about the close relationships that formed among a group of players united in their pursuit of common goals. Others emphasized the ways playing sports at a high level encouraged their children to develop skills like perseverance and resilience that would be valuable to them throughout their lives. As would be expected, they also appreciated the athletic progress their sons and daughters made as a result of the heightened level of play associated with travel sports. The relative importance assigned to these factors varied significantly from parent to parent.

It was also challenging to draw any conclusions about a parent's priorities with certainty. The frequent inconsistencies and contradictions they made suggested that most were not completely sure what they ultimately wanted for their children. Parents often seemed to be searching for clarity themselves. Even after monitoring their sons' and daughters' athletic activities for years, they were plagued by indecision. What began as a fairly straightforward exercise—providing children with opportunities to play and grow— became more muddled as their children got older. The goal of creating opportunities for their sons and daughters was distorted in response to competing messages about athletic excellence, achievement, personal satisfaction, and effective parenting.

Recent expansion of the youth sports industry has made the process of overseeing a child's athletic development more challenging. Young athletes and their families are pressed to commit to year-round athletics at the stage when, a generation ago, many kids were signing up to play organized sports for the first time. Failure to follow this early specialization trend could jeopardize a young athlete's future prospects, at least in the minds of some parents. This ambiguity, combined with a desire to do what's best for a child, creates pressure to constantly increase the stakes of their investment in their child's athletic career. In this way, signing up children for additional training sessions, trying out for higher level teams, and attending more showcase events all represent forms of insurance for uncertain parents.

The longer athletes and their families participate in travel sports, the greater the pressure to accept this "more is more" way of thinking. In response, parents often change from amenable supporters of their children's sports activities to career managers. Turning down any potential opportunities becomes difficult. Furthermore, as families advance through the youth sports system, the people they interact with most often tend to have accepted this view. In such an environment, a college athletic scholarship represents the ultimate mark of success. In reality, fewer than 10 percent of all high school athletes will eventually play sports in college. Nevertheless, the number of young athletes aspiring for NCAA careers continues to grow, and their parents are encouraged to do whatever they can to make that dream a reality.

CHAPTER THREE

To Specialize or Not to Specialize

That Is the Question

"So parents are really pushing their children to be outstanding at age six. So they leave practice and they go to a private coach and train and they're making merchandise and already just trying to promote their child and make sure that child gets enough playing time, gets enough exposure. And it's real competitive. And that's just to get social media attention—to get whatever kind of attention possible. They just want to put their child in the front."

— Youth coach and parent —

"I was a three-sport athlete in high school, and I played club soccer and AAU basketball. That is no longer the situation. . . . Having the ability to play three sports and just the different experiences you have with different coaches, different sports, different teammates in different venues even . . . I think that's the big change that's happening, we're going in a direction where you're not allowed to do other things, especially once you get to be of high school age."

— College soccer coach —

When we were kids, athletes tended to play several sports a year for a few months each. The costs were minimal and the stakes low. After soccer season ended, a player moved on to basketball or gymnastics or music. They might even take a few months off before beginning the next extracurricular activity. That was true of kids who played sports mainly to spend time with their friends as well as elite athletes. Sports was something kids did because they enjoyed it, not because they hoped to earn a scholarship to play sports in college. And for those who did plan to play sports in college, earning awards based on their performance on a high school team was enough to get the attention of college scouts. Parents did not feel compelled to manage their children's athletic careers. All that was required of them was to show up at games and cheer for their kids.

Things have changed. Dramatically. Over a relatively short period of time. For many parents, the world of youth sports today looks nothing like what they experienced as kids. At younger and younger ages, kids are feeling pressure to dedicate themselves to a single sport and to play that sport year-round. The push to specialize can hit when a kid is only seven or eight years old. Sometimes, kids make that decision themselves—an elementary school student wants to play for a travel team because her friends are on that club or she relishes the competition that comes with playing on an elite team. In other cases, the parents decide that their son will benefit from year-round play; joining a travel league will give them access to higher quality coaching than would be provided in a recreational league.

In either case, parents will need to make difficult decisions and those decisions are likely to have unintended consequences. As we have emphasized in previous chapters, joining a team that plays throughout the year places demands on all members of a family. Simply transporting a young athlete to multiple practices and games a week can be challenging, especially if a team competes against clubs from other cities and regions. The financial demands can also be considerable. The costs associated with joining a privately run club are likely to be exponentially higher than participating in a town-based-recreational league. And those costs escalate as an athlete gets older. Parents as well as siblings are likely to be affected by the increased demands. As one mother we interviewed shared, "My daughter plays on an elite softball team. She's a really good player and could probably make it to a higher level. But she's happy where she is and that's okay with us. Still, we pay a lot of money to the league. You can't believe how expensive it gets. And she's not even playing at the highest level."

If you ask an MLB star's parents if the sacrifices they made were worth it, they will probably say yes—without taking a second to think about it. The potential payoffs can be enticing. Why not fork out a few thousand dollars if there is a potential pay out of millions down the line? Doesn't it make sense to go all-in with sports if a child might eventually rise to the highest levels of the athletic hierarchy? The answers to these questions will depend on a family's values and goals. Our motivation for writing this chapter was not to lobby for any type of sports activity over another. Rather, we wanted to provide parents with information that will help them make sensible decisions for their children.

As we were conducting the research for this book, we discovered that when parents are unsure of what activities to sign up their children for, they tend to follow the crowd. When faced with uncertainty, they rely on their friends for direction. If a particular team is popular among kids in the neighborhood, they sign up their own child to try out for that club. In many cases, this works out. But in some instances, parents later regret the decisions they make. After a season or two, they discover their child enjoys swimming but doesn't really want to spend three hours in a pool every day, twelve months a year. Or maybe they lose interest in a particular sport. After all, kids tend to change their minds about lots of things when they are young. Making long-term plans based on the things they like to do when they are eight doesn't make a lot of sense. Nevertheless, kids today feel a great deal of pressure to specialize in a single sport as early as possible—and many of their parents encourage that. As one father told us, "We learned that my son is already behind because he's nine years old and just started playing hockey, which is absurd. I didn't start playing soccer until my freshman year of high school, and I was able to play soccer in college. It was just D3, but it was college soccer. I really appreciated my experience. I got to do so many different things. But when I see what my kid is going through, it makes me worry."

In the sections that follow, we share information we hope will give parents a better sense of the reasons why so many young athletes are specializing in a single sport. We discuss the effects sports specialization has on a young athletes physical, social, and mental development. We hope this material will provide a valuable balance to any rumors that are circulating through their social circles or on social media. The more information parents have, the more likely they are to make decisions that will benefit their kids in the long run.

Shifting Norms and Expectations

Prior to the 1980s, most youth sports programs were publicly funded and community-based. In elementary school, kids tended to play several different sports for short spurts of time. As they entered adolescence, athletes often signed up to play for school teams. The costs of participating were minimal and a sports season typically lasted three to four months. This structure created a natural flow to children's lives; they shifted from one activity to another at several points during the year.

During the last two decades of the twentieth century, cuts in government funding spurred widespread changes in the athletic activities provided to children. Reduced funding for local parks and recreation departments created a gap that needed to be filled. In addition, plummeting tax revenues led many school districts to reduce or eliminate many after-school sports. This situation created an opening that sports entrepreneurs filled. They created privately run programs that charged participation fees to parents looking for activities to keep their children busy. Some of those commercial organizations offered services they marketed as complementary to school-based sports, while others billed themselves as superior alternatives to scholastic teams. Sports entrepreneurs also offered specialized services, charging fees for families to enroll their children in high performance training, private coaching, and year-round competition that drew participants from multiple cities.

Another segment of the commercialized sports marketplace that became popular were tournaments that drew teams from across different regions and states to compete for prizes and recognition. These tournaments, which are now organized in virtually every part of the country, vary in size and intensity. For example, a town near us sponsors a Columbus Day Soccer Tournament for travel soccer teams located within an hour's drive or so. Families arrive early in the morning, play a few games, and get home before dinner. Teams interested in more serious competition with loftier aspirations apply to participate in competitions offered at Dreams Park in Cooperstown or the ESPN Wide World of Sports Complex at Disneyworld. The costs of taking part in high level tournaments can include entry fees, hotel stays, and airplane tickets. They attract the interest—and dollars—of families from around the country eager to certify the status of their children as elite athletes. Sports tourism has evolved into a multibillion-dollar industry.[9]

It became increasingly common for athletes (and their parents) to seek ways to distinguish themselves from potential competitors. Youth sports increasingly became privatized, costly, performance-oriented, and regionally centered. For many athletes, playing for their school is no longer considered adequate. At younger and younger ages, athletes are encouraged to sign up and pay for activities that have the potential to enhance their athletic profiles. Privately run sports clubs provide intense training that might set participants apart from their peers—but also demand a great deal of them, physically and mentally. In many cases, they expect athletes to dedicate themselves to playing a single sport year-round. Parents frequently accept this situation out of concern that their children might lose their competitive edge if they decide not to specialize. The consequences of following this pathway should not be underestimated.

Effects of Specialization

In the 1980s and 1990s, when most contemporary parents played sports themselves, knowledge about specialization was limited—because it was a relatively rare phenomenon. Over the last two decades, however, researchers, physicians, and journalists have started to pay close attention to the effects of sports specialization. The reports they have published provide a detailed picture of the costs and benefits associated with playing a single sport intensely.

Specialists who study child development have identified three primary ways that playing sports affect young athletes. The most obvious is the benefits to physical health that athletics provide. Physical activity can promote cardiovascular fitness, muscular strength and endurance, and weight control. In addition, playing sports can support children's psychosocial development; athletes learn important life skills, such as cooperation, leadership, discipline, and self-control. Third, youth sports help participants learn valuable motor skills. Furthermore, the physical activities that athletes develop in childhood are associated with their habits in adulthood.[10]

Clearly, kids can benefit from being physically active. However, it is important to recognize the positive outcomes of playing sports are not automatic. A team of scholars from Queen's University in Canada emphasize that "there appears to be a void between the potential positive outcomes, and some of the negative realities of youth sports programs."[11] Athletes who start to specialize in a single sport at a young age are especially likely to suffer those negative consequences. Playing a single sport intensely for sustained period times can produce physical stress that many young bodies are not prepared to handle. This can counteract the benefits of physical activity that we mention above.

When kids move from one physical activity to another, they engage different parts of their bodies. This distributes pressure across the various muscle groups and reduces the chances of injury. But when an athlete plays the same sport day after day throughout the year, the muscles that are most actively engaged may get little rest. This can lead to overuse injuries that can be quite debilitating, especially for children. According to a sports psychologist we interviewed, "The physical impact of this is huge. Kids who specialize in one sport are more likely to get injured. That's pretty obvious. And it extends beyond sports. If you're playing sports all of the time, you're not learning other skills. You're not developing as much as a human being."

Single sport specialization has been associated with increased risk of injury to knees, shoulders, elbows, and ankles. For preadolescent athletes, the effects of those injuries can be long lasting. A report published by the National Federation of State High School Associations concludes that athletes who are highly specialized have an 85 percent increased risk of injury compared to athletes who choose to participate in multiple sports throughout the year.[12] Recognizing the increase in youth sport specialization in recent years, a physical therapist we interviewed explained, "It is so much more common for kids to play year-round on multiple travel teams and prioritize their specific sport over other activities. It is ever so common for children who lack movement diversification to end up at our clinic due to a lack of recovery and overuse." Year-round training also tends to emphasize the improvement of specific athletic skills rather than on exercise designed to improve core physical fitness.

Some organizations have taken steps to address these issues. For example, Little League sets a maximum number of pitches that players can throw in a game. Once they meet that limit, pitchers are required to switch to another position. While this is a step in the right direction, its impact is limited when individuals play for multiple teams or receive supplemental coaching. Pitching in a Little League game may represent only a fraction of the activities that place strain on a child's arm during the week. And given the structure of youth sports today, young athletes may not have the luxury of taking a few weeks off at the end of a season. The physical demands placed on their bodies can be relentless.

The growing popularity of commercial, privately run clubs has exacerbated the situation. As the competition for attention has increased, so have the demands placed on athletes. A kid who hopes to become an all-star may find it difficult to turn down opportunities that may take a toll on their bodies. A desire to give their children a leg up on potential competitors can also blind adults to the costs of sports specialization. The physical therapist we interviewed described the challenges of educating parents about the factors that contribute to pediatric sports injuries: "They are typically receptive to this education. However, they often are hesitant to implement the advice due to fear of missing out on important scouting or development opportunities, fear of their child falling behind in their sport relative to their peers who specialize, as well as the notion that year-round sports specialization is the only way for their child to make a future high school, college, or professional team." In an environment in which elementary school-aged kids are traveling to different states to participate in elite tournaments, maintaining a sense of balance can be challenging.

Mental Health Considerations

The decision of whether or not to specialize can also affect an athlete's mental health. As we mention above, participating in organized sports can boost a child's self-esteem and sense of belonging. Playing sports provides opportunities for children to develop bonds with other athletically minded kids. The competition provided can push them to become more focused, set goals for themselves, and learn how to work with all different kinds of kids. The players and parents we interviewed highlighted the social and emotional benefits tied to playing competitive sports. One theme of those interviews was the strength girls derived through athletics.

Parents told us that on the field, their daughters didn't have to compete with boys, which gave them a chance to hold leadership positions that were not available to them in other settings.

There is no doubt that sports can support children's social and emotional development. However, it is also important to recognize that specializing in a single sport at a young age may have negative consequences for developing athletes. One common concern among specialists who study this topic relates to the satisfaction children derive from playing sports. What often drives kids to begin participating in a sport is their love for the game. But if they start training intensely at a young age, athletes often lose interest in a sport. As we have noted, participating in a travel sports program places more extensive demands on athletes than is true of most recreational leagues. Players are required to dedicate more time and attention to the team. They spend more time practicing and face higher levels of competition. The pressure to win can be intense. As one coach told us, "Youth sports is not going in the direction it should in terms of the health of children. You can develop a love of sports and continue that for life, but if you don't, you burn out. A lot of kids are burning out."

Research indicates that children who take sports seriously often feel a sense of failure when they do not accomplish their goals. If they are involved in a recreational league with a short season, that pressure is less severe. It is easier for a player to downplay any setbacks they experience. But the time and effort athletes invest in year-round sports tend to amplify the pressures they experience. In response to those pressures, they may start to question their abilities, feel low levels of self-confidence, and have conflicts with their teammates.[13] In more extreme cases, they can become anxious, depressed, or develop eating disorders.[14] This is true of individuals who excel on the field as well as those who are less successful. In the games that we observed, it was often the star players who had trouble managing their emotions. Rather than work cooperatively with their teammates, they lashed out at players who they felt had let them down.

Research indicates the pressure to perform, combined with severe injuries, increases the risk of mental illness among athletes.[15] Comments that parents shared with us back up this reality. As one father told us, "I just think from a mental health perspective, when you get focused on one sport and everyone tells you how great you are at it, there's a lot of pressure for you to succeed in that sport as a player. I think there's a lot of pressure put on these kids from so many other aspects of life. The last thing they need is pressure from sports." A coach we interviewed expressed a similar opinion: "The mental health part is important . . . the pressure to succeed can actually break them and hinder them from succeeding in other areas of life."

Some kids thrive under pressure. They use the demands associated with sports as a source of motivation. When confronted with difficult circumstances, they push themselves to perform, to overcome obstacles, to defeat formidable opponents. We often hear reports about those inspiring competitors. But not all individuals thrive in those circumstances. For many young athletes, the pressure to perform can be overwhelming. When young athletes feel inadequate, they may become withdrawn, self-critical, or depressed. For those kids, sports become a source of stress rather than pleasure. The number one reason kids decide to stop playing a sport? "I was not having fun" (followed closely by "I had a health problem or injury").[16] This happens more often than you may think. Approximately 70 percent of children drop out of organized sports before the age of thirteen.[17]

It's easy to overlook young athletes who are quietly suffering. They tend not to draw attention to themselves—and adults don't always spot the signs of unhappiness. Parents may not want to acknowledge that playing sports has become a negative force in their children's lives. Facing that reality can be difficult. Yet research indicates that mental distress among young athletes is on the rise.

The Competitive Edge

Given the risks of specializing in a single sport, why do so many families opt to sign up their kid to play for teams that place such extensive demands on players? In many cases, parents don't have a good understanding of the implications of that decision. They simply follow the lead of other people they know. In other cases, playing for a team that is considered elite feeds the dreams they have for their child. Any child can sign up to play AYSO soccer, but earning a spot on a team that competes against clubs from other cities or regions signifies that their kid is special. According to this logic, if an eight-year-old earns a spot on a travel team, they are on the pathway to great things. That could be the first step toward earning an athletic scholarship or maybe even a professional career. After all, according to one common saying, it takes 10,000 hours of effort to become an expert in any type of activity. If that is the case, why not start banking those hours when a child is young?

What many parents don't realize is that for most sports, intense training at an early age is not necessary to achieve elite status.[18] A team of physicians who studied this issue concluded, "For most sports, there is no evidence that intense training and specialization before puberty are necessary to achieve elite status."[19] Sampling many sports may actually increase the chances that a person will excel in sports later in life. Studies that document the careers of college and professional athletes support this claim. For example, NCAA Division I athletes are more likely to have played multiple sports in high school than those who compete in a single sport year-round. On average, Division I athletes do not specialize in a single sport until the ages of fourteen to fifteen.[20] And the majority of female athletes who compete at the NCAA level had their first organized sport experiences in a sport other than the sport they focus on in college.[21] This pattern applies to professional athletes as well. For example, of the athletes who participated in a recent NFL scouting combine, 87 percent played in multiple sports in high school.[22]

A strong body of research supports the idea that for most sports, early diversification and late specialization is a dependable route to elite status. Parents may not realize this, but coaches do. The vast majority of youth sport coaches report that playing multiple sports during childhood is the most effective way to nurture athletic ability.[23]

This makes a great deal of sense, if we think about the way children develop physically and psychologically. Playing multiple sports allows athletes to develop different muscle groups without putting excessive stress on a particular muscle group; it also supports flexibility. The skills learned in one sport are likely to transfer to other sports. One study conducted by a team of physicians concluded that the greater number of activities athletes participate in before reaching the age of twelve, the less sport-specific practice was necessary for them to become experts in a single sport in high school.[24] Developing a wide range of athletic skills when athletes are young may ultimately provide them with the competitive edges their parents are seeking.

Seeking Solutions

Conducting research and applying the findings to real life situations are two different things. How should parents interpret all this information about the effects of sports specialization? We want to emphasize that specialization in and of itself is not bad. Investing a great deal of effort into a single sport can lead to success on the athletic field. However, decisions about if and when to specialize should be taken seriously.

Timing is key. The consensus among researchers, physicians, and athletic trainers is that children should not take part in intense or specialized training before the age of twelve. Sampling multiple sports at a young age is likely to provide them with more enjoyment, fewer injuries, and long-term success on the athletic field. Taking this approach will help children develop a range of skills they can apply to whatever sport they decide to focus on when they are in high school or college. Most of the parents of young athletes we interviewed did not realize this. When they made decisions, the desire to make their children stand out from the competition seemed to trump all other factors. Parents of older children, on the other hand, were more likely to recognize the benefits of delaying specialization. Having observed their children's interests in various sports shift over time, more seasoned parents recognized the benefits of allowing kids to experiment before dedicating themselves to a single endeavor. In a sense, they came to view the world of youth sports through a wide-angle lens.

One important step parents can take throughout their children's athletic careers is to establish open lines of communication. Talking about sports on a regular basis will help parents get a sense of whether an athlete is still motivated to participate in a particular sport or if they are doing so out of a sense of obligation. If a kid no longer looks forward to attending practices or games, parents should offer them an exit ramp, making it clear that taking a break from a particular sport or activity is an acceptable option. Children should feel they can make choices about their athletic careers without fear of being judged.[25] Maintaining an open dialogue will help parents assess their children's mental health and make decisions that are in their long-term best interests.

As we have emphasized, decisions about whether or not to specialize, at what age this might make sense, and how much emphasis to place on sports will vary depending on the individual athlete's needs and interests. However, several professional organizations have published concrete guidelines that parents can follow as they oversee their children's athletic careers. For example, the National Trainer's Association offers the following recommendations related to the health and well-being of young athletes:

- Delay sport specializing in a single sport for as long as possible.

- Participate in one organized sport per season.

- Adolescent and young athletes should not play a single sport for more than eight months per year.

- Athletes should not participate in organized sports for more hours per week than their age.

- Adolescents should have a minimum of two days off per week from organized training and competition.

- Athletes should spend time away from organized sports at the end of each competitive season.

Following this advice will reduce the likelihood of injury or burnout.

Predicting what an individual will accomplish as an athlete based on their performance as a seven-year-old is a futile exercise. A child who excels on the softball field may turn into a star pitcher in college—or may lose interest in the sport and decide their passion is swimming or gymnastics or student government. This is why sampling makes so much sense for most young athletes. They need time to just be kids without having to worry about the long-term consequences of any decisions they make.

The American Psychiatric Association has published a series of reports that discuss the impact playing sports has on children today. Those reports emphasize the importance of helping young athletes find a balance between their sports commitments and their sense of well-being. Kids should be encouraged to take breaks, relax, and participate in a variety of activities.[26] If children are mentored in this way, they are more likely to discover what makes them feel most fulfilled and successful. In a society that often places a premium on public displays of accomplishment, it is easy to lose sight of this message. Trying to create children who are exceptional may not be in their best interests.

CHAPTER FOUR

Scholarship Dreams

College Sports Myths and Meanings

"They [his high school teammates] all got to play ball. They're all playing at college, even people who aren't as good as him got picked to play at colleges. So, in that case he feels that we did it wrong and we didn't invest enough in him."

— High school baseball parent —

"You probably know that of those that actually go onto college and get onto a roster, that you look at the end . . . a significant percentage either play very little or drop off of the team. The number that actually came in as freshmen that end up as seniors having played and participated on the team for four years is relatively, not small, but there's another chunk of people that get lost along the way. So many high school seniors, how many end up being college seniors playing? It's a pretty big drop off. That's something kids don't understand and parents don't understand."

— College soccer coach —

Playing competitive sports is very much an in-the-moment activity; in order to succeed, young athletes must learn to focus on the current shot, pass, or pitch. More sophisticated players may be able to anticipate an opponent's or teammate's next move, but generally speaking, sports demand that they focus on the task at hand and avoid the tendency to think too far ahead. Many parents of young athletes value sports precisely because it is an activity where kids learn to concentrate, a highly valued life skill. Staying in the moment is, in many respects, a key component of athletic success; it is also an important part of what brings joy to sports.

At the same time, youth sport is a surprisingly future-oriented enterprise. As we discussed in Chapter One, the dramatic growth of travel sports programs is driven, in part, by parents who want their kids to succeed—and definitions of success are almost entirely focused on future athletic opportunities. A growing number of young athletes train year-round, work with private coaches, and attend intense instructional summer camps in hopes of improving so they can play at an even higher level. For younger kids, the goal may simply be making the travel team roster. But there always seems to be another level of play to aspire to: a select tournament team, a premier or elite team, a regional or national team, or one's high school team. A similar dynamic exists for some travel teams, which may keep a core roster of the same players as they seek to move on to more advanced levels of competition, often culminating in trips to travel tournaments branded as "nationals" in a given sport.

Even as parents and coaches often stress how important it is to learn to focus, the youth sports scene is shaped, paradoxically, by an underlying emphasis on what's next. Many kids, even those still in elementary school, face implicit questions about what they will get in return, how they will benefit from playing sports. Perhaps such questions seem a natural response to the substantial time, money, and emotional energy so many families invest in youth sports. Nonetheless, it is puzzling that so many adults—from parents and grandparents to coaches and local sports reporters—

see youth sports in instrumental terms. Where will sports take you? How will you benefit? What's next?

While many young athletes may fantasize about a future professional career—and given the cultural visibility and celebrity status of contemporary professional athletes, who can blame kids for dreaming of stardom—parents typically focus on a different goal: playing college sports.

In the world of youth sports, where players compete in a steady stream of tournaments and often play two or three "seasons" each year, team goals of winning championships often take a back seat to a player's individual accomplishments: being named to all-star teams or selected to play on elite team clubs are evidence of a player's (and, by extension, a family's) achievements. The most widely discussed and sought after goal—a kind of Holy Grail in youth sports circles—is becoming a college athlete. If you spend any time around youth sports parents, you will quickly recognize the intensity of the appeal of college sports. "I hope my son can play at the college level, even if it's only for his own recreation," one parent explained to us. Another person volunteered that "I would have nothing against her playing club ball in college, but I don't want it to be her focus. There are so many parents whose attitude is like 'Whatever it takes to get them an offer.' I'm on the other side." As these comments indicate, parents have a wide range of opinions about the topic, but almost everyone has an opinion about the subject they are willing to share.

It is a peculiar feature of kids' sports that so much conversation and energy is focused on playing in college. Outside of big-time college football and basketball, which have lucrative television deals and are a major cultural presence, most college sports attract little public attention and offer few financial rewards to players. Nevertheless, hoping to play in college is a broadly shared goal in youth sports communities, one that is discussed regularly among parents and players, even though the vast majority of youth athletes will never play collegiate sports.

Interest in playing college sports is so deeply embedded in contemporary youth sports that it extends to the youngest players. Many parents of very young athletes hope—or expect—their children will play college sports. In our survey of travel sports parents, more than half of parents (55.5 percent) responded that they thought it was "likely" or "very likely" their child would play on a collegiate sports team. And this view of the future doesn't just exist for parents of older players who are actively considering college. Among parents of the youngest athletes, age ten and under, 57 percent of parents thought their child was "likely" or "very likely" to play in college. This last statistic is particularly striking, given that the athletes in question had most likely been playing organized sports for only two or three years.

Although some youth athletes do play sports in college, the likelihood of playing in college is far lower than most people think. Still, the allure of college sports lurks ubiquitously around youth sports. We have found commentary about college sports—during formal interviews with parents and players, watching practices and games, milling about with parents on the sidelines, and listening to player chatter—to be so common as to be a kind of near-constant background buzz. Such talk includes descriptions of conversations with college coaches, visits to college campuses, and experiences at college showcase events. In fact, much parent and player commentary on college prospects revolves around tales, typically second or third hand, of the college opportunities of other, often older, players. Stories abound about players who are getting lots of attention from college coaches, have been promised roster spots, or have received scholarship offers.

Some of these stories are likely true, at least in part, but the information circulates in a way that makes it difficult for anyone to know the full story. The constant talk of who's going where only serves to reinforce just how important it is to try to play in college. It can also shape the identity and actions of parents. When adults are constantly surrounded by conversations about the prospects of advancing to the NCAA, parents may find it difficult to resist this possibility, even if it is not in their children's best interests.

How College Became the Goal

There is no simple explanation for how playing sports in college became such a common aspiration for young athletes. Certainly, it has not always been this way. College athletics played a much smaller role in childhood dreams as recently as a generation ago. How can we understand the forces driving the widespread adoption of college sports as a desired next step?

First, we should recognize the high (and continuously growing) cost of college. One powerful driver of the college sports dream is the widely believed idea that players who excel in sports will receive an athletic scholarship to help pay for college. Even though the odds of receiving a substantial athletic scholarship are quite low, the very possibility, as well as the incomplete and sometimes largely fictitious stories of other scholarship athletes, helps scholarship dreams to thrive.

Our parent survey found that more than one-quarter of parents, 28 percent, believe it is "very likely" or "likely" their child will receive an athletic scholarship. Among those parents who say their child is "very likely" to play college sports, a substantial majority, 59 percent, believe their child will receive an athletic scholarship. These collective parental assessments stand in stark contrast to the reality that only about one in 100 high school athletes receive a sports scholarship to play in college.

The economic and cultural value of a college degree continues to grow, as does the cost of a college education. In this context, many middle-class parents struggle to figure out how they can afford to send their kids to college; working class and poor families often face even tougher challenges related to the cost of college. When a child excels as a young athlete, many parents think sports might just be the ticket to help pay for college. Paying substantial amounts of money for a child's sports activities—and the travel, training, and instruction aimed at growing a player's skills—

becomes an investment in the future, with a presumed payoff of an athletic scholarship. The hope and dream of playing in college is, at least in part, a way for parents to both rationalize their youth sports spending and answer the just-beneath-the-surface "what's the value of sports" question. The 2024 settlement of the class action lawsuit, House v. NCAA, which provides for payments to football and men's and women's basketball players in the "Power 5" conferences, as well as recent developments permitting collegiate players to receive money for endorsements in the form of "Name, Image, and Likeness" (NIL) payments, are likely to increase parent and player dreams of a potential future payday.

Potential financial rewards are only part of the explanation of the college sports dream. Playing a sport in college often confers a valuable form of status on both players and parents. Those who achieve the goal of playing at the next level are commonly recognized by their schools, their club teams, and within their communities for their achievement. Parents of college-bound athletes, similarly, receive congratulations within extended social networks and reap often short-lived status rewards of having successfully shepherded a child into college athletics.

College-bound athletes often benefit from substantial public support within their communities, and this can be a satisfying form of recognition of a young athlete's many years of hard work. Newspapers regularly include short articles that highlight local athletes advancing into the college ranks, often including updates on their athletic accomplishments during their college years. Travel programs, especially those that market themselves as college development programs, regularly feature up-to-date lists of colleges where program alum went off to play. And high schools frequently highlight graduates who are moving on to play sports in college at school assemblies and on school websites and newsletters.

X (formerly known as Twitter) is full of photos of players with their coaches and parents on the day they "sign" to play at a specific college. National Letters of Intent (NLI) for Division 1 college athletes are, effectively, when players commit to a specific school, accepting a coach's offer of a full or partial scholarship. Signing an NLI tells your future college that you will attend and lets other college coaches know they can no longer recruit you. Interestingly, in recent years, many Division 3 athletes have taken to staging signing ceremonies, even though athletic scholarships are not permitted and players are effectively indicating which college, among those where they've been offered admission, they plan to attend. For high school athletes, the signing ceremony is a way for college-bound athletes to announce to their community— former coaches and teammates, younger athletes in the community, parents and teachers with whom they have worked—that they have achieved their goal of playing in the NCAA.

For young athletes and their families, this kind of recognition provides a kind of public acknowledgment of success, even before a player has ever worn their college uniform. It confirms that effort and dedication have paid off and gives the next crop of young athletes hope that they, too, can work their way onto a college roster. It reaffirms for just about everyone in the youth sports ecosystem that the dream, whatever form it may take, is alive. The letter signing ceremony confirms for parents, in a very public setting, that the years of shuttling their children to practices, games, tournaments, and showcases were worth it.

External Influences

The dream of playing sports in college is stoked aggressively by participants in a growing college recruiting industry that both promotes the goal of playing in college and offers fee-based services to help players "be recruited," as one popular online recruiting network is called. These recruiting services take many forms, but what they share is an approach that feeds the dream of playing a college sport.

Elite "college development" teams are perhaps the most fully developed of these services. By the time a player reaches high school, some travel sports programs announce themselves as college development teams; they aim to help players improve their skills and promise to leverage program contacts and high-visibility tournaments to get players seen by the right college coaches. Some of these programs are remarkably expensive, running $10,000 to $15,000 per year for the most travel-heavy teams. Certainly, some programs have a track record of success with many of their players heading off to play in college. Many other programs have limited success, but having just a handful of alum on college rosters can entice enthusiastic families to sign on to those travel teams. In any case, most of these college development teams emphasize securing roster spots over academic opportunities with questions about post-college (and post-sports) life plans often fading into the background.

Other, typically less expensive, promoters of the dream include paid college recruiting consultants and online recruiting services. Recruiting consultants provide highly individualized services for young athletes; at their best, such consultants can help families sort through options, identify what's realistic from a sports standpoint, and help players think through the complex relationship between college athletics and academics. Typically, however, academics are not a central focus, as recruiting consultants face pressure to affirm player and parent dreams about athletic achievement, if only because their income depends in large part on the reproduction of that dream. As a result, recruiting consultants are successful when they "place" players on a college team, often regardless of whether it is the best fit for the student athlete. Recruiting consultants build successful businesses by developing relationships with a recurring set of college coaches to whom they can consistently deliver recruits. Most players and parents are not aware of how all of this works when they write a multi-thousand-dollar check to a recruiting consultant who promises they can deliver the scarce commodity of college coach attention.

Recruiting websites are less expensive ways for players to get attention from coaches. Websites such as Berecruited.com, CaptainU.com, and SportsRecruits.com—three of the many such services—all tell student athletes they will help connect prospective players with college coaches, offering tips on how to communicate with coaches and hosting promotional player-specific sites full of stats, testimonials, academic information, and a recruiting video (which is often produced, for a fee, by a third-party video production partner).

To be sure, most of these recruiting services are above board. They are not hucksters preying on youthful (or parental) dreams. And many can demonstrate a track record of helping their clients play in college. Still, the existence of this industry is premised on the widespread dream of playing sports in college, so it should be no surprise that the college recruiting industry offers subtle and not-so-subtle endorsements of the dream. One company offering highlight video production services for use in recruiting promotes itself with the tagline "If you started in high school, you can play in college," wildly overestimating the chances of playing a college sport. Another leading online recruiting business markets its services by encouraging prospective users to "Create your online athletic recruiting profile to maximize your college recruiting exposure and sports scholarship opportunities." For the aspiring athlete and their parents, who are often uninformed about college sports, such promotional language can have a powerful impact on their plans. Recruiting services affirm the family's sports dreams, counseling them on what they need to do (and pay) to maximize their chance of achieving that goal.

Given the alignment of forces that inspire the dream of playing in college, it is important to note that few young athletes experience this dream as something thrust upon them. For most student athletes, the goal of playing in college is a genuine desire, one born of the joy of competitive sports, plenty of success and affirmation in their chosen sport, perhaps even a sense of identity. Many of the young athletes who express a desire to play in college are, fundamentally, seeking an opportunity to continue to play a sport that has been a central part of their childhood. Playing another year—or another four years—is reason enough to embrace the roller-coaster ride of college recruiting, to chase a dream they may, at least in moments, know is a long shot, and to persevere in the face of uncertainty and the pressure associated with marketing oneself.

Lurking in the background of the college athletics dream is the recognition that, sooner or later (and sooner for most young athletes), the final game will arrive. This is by no means a tragedy, but for kids who have played competitive sports for much of their childhood, and for their parents, who have coached, cheered, and driven, playing a college sport offers a way to delay the inevitable transition to a new stage of life. Perhaps that is one reason why so much anxiety surrounds articulations of the college sports dream.

Reality Check: Who Plays College Sports

Dreams are typically not subject to rational evaluation. They persist even in the face of great uncertainty and long odds. In this respect, the college sports dream is no different from other youthful dreams. What's interesting is how long the dream persists—often well into high school—and how deeply so many young athletes and their parents believe their dream is, in fact, a sensible assessment of the future.

There is plenty of publicly available information about who plays college sports. And for all of those young athletes and parents who are planning on future college athletics, the numbers can be demoralizing. The odds of playing college sports are low; the vast majority of young athletes will never compete in the NCAA. Data on the likelihood of participating in college athletics is clear and sobering. Only about 7 percent of high school athletes—or about one in thirteen—go on to play a varsity sport in college, and less than 2 percent (one in fifty-seven) of high school athletes play in a Division 1 college program.[27] The NCAA reports that only 3.6 percent of male high school basketball players earn a roster spot on a college basketball team, and only 1 percent play for a Division 1 program. The figures are slightly higher for women's basketball—4.5 percent play in college, with 1.8 percent playing at a Division 1 program—with the difference largely a result of there being many fewer female than male high school basketball players. While there is considerable variation by sport, the likelihood of playing college sports, especially at the Division 1 level, is considerably lower than many families believe.

The low probability of playing in college, however, is typically absent from most parent conversations about youth sports, at least until disappointment sets in for young athletes who find the route to playing in college is a much harder road than they had been led to believe. When parents are aware of the low odds, they often choose to ignore what they hear, telling themselves their child is among the few who will successfully navigate the road to playing in college. Some parents are so confident their child will earn a Division I scholarship that they are skeptical, even dismissive, of the prospect of a Division II or III opportunity, even though the total number of Division II and III athletes is far greater than the number of Division I athletes (see Table 3).

Table 1
Probability a High School Athlete Will Compete in College by Sport (Men)

Sport	Division 1	Divisions I, II, III
Baseball	2.4%	8.1%
Basketball	1.0%	3.6%
Football	3.0%	7.5%
Lacrosse	3.3%	14.4%
Soccer	1.4%	6.1%
Tennis	1.5%	4.8%

Source: NCAA (2024)

Table 2
Probability a High School Athlete Will Compete in College by Sport (Women)

Sport	Division 1	Divisions I, II, III
Basketball	1.4%	4.5%
Lacrosse	4.3%	13.8%
Soccer	2.7%	7.9%
Softball	2.0%	6.3%
Tennis	1.5%	4.4%
Volleyball	1.2%	3.9%

Source: NCAA (2024)

Table 3
Number of NCAA College Athletes by Division, 2022–23

2022–23	Number of Athletes Division 1	Percent of Total Athletes	Number of Athletes Divisions II and III	Percent of Total Athletes
Male	102,531	34%	199,037	66%
Female	89,537	39%	141,414	61%

Source: NCAA Sports Sponsorship and Participation Rates Report (September 29, 2023)

Since most Division 1 schools have far fewer scholarships than roster spots, the odds of receiving a substantial college scholarship are lower still. In fact, most athletes outside of major college football and basketball receive partial, rather than full, athletic scholarships, making the likelihood of getting a "free ride" to college through an athletic scholarship incredibly rare; according to the NCSA College Recruiting, fewer than 2 percent of high school athletes receive college scholarships, and only 1 percent are offered a full scholarship.[28] Despite the very low odds, the belief that a young athlete is on track for a "ride" remains prevalent and persists—even when there are strong signals conveying these very low odds—among the parents of young athletes.

Part of what makes the scholarship picture so opaque to most parents and prospective players is a general misunderstanding about the availability of athletic scholarships. Again, the cultural prominence of big-time college football and basketball, the sports that generate most of the athletic revenue for the NCAA and its member colleges, gives a false impression of the funds available for student athletes. Take, for example, major college football. The NCAA allows each team within its top tier Football Bowl Subdivision (FBS) a maximum of eighty-five scholarships. With more than 130 teams in the FBS, this means there are more than 11,000 football scholarships at big-time college football programs. Even though many college football rosters reach 100 players or more, the eighty-five-scholarship limit means that even third and fourth string players, those who might never see the field on game day, are supported by an athletic scholarship.

Similarly, Division 1 women's basketball permits fifteen scholarship players and men's basketball permits thirteen scholarship players, which means that major college basketball rosters are populated almost exclusively with players on athletic scholarships. In major college sports, we hear occasional stories of players who are "walk-ons," nonscholarship athletes, but success among walk-ons is extremely rare, and success almost always results in becoming a scholarship player the next year. Yet media accounts often highlight walk-ons who earn spots on college teams, which feeds the idea that anyone can make it to the NCAA if they work hard enough. In fact, it can be difficult to "walk on" to many Division 3 programs, since coaches have already built relationships with and made commitments to a recruiting class that often already exceeds the available number of roster spots.

Football and basketball, however, are different from other Division 1 college sports, where scholarships are far less plentiful. In fact, in most other sports there are far more players on a team roster than there are available scholarships, so most Division 1 athletes outside of football and basketball receive partial scholarships at best. In baseball, for example, the NCAA permits a total of 11.7 scholarships for each Division 1 team. With an average roster size of forty, baseball teams have the equivalent of more than three players for each scholarship. As a result, scholarships are chopped up into pieces, with more desirable recruits receiving larger chunks and some players receiving no scholarship money at all.

The situation is similar for many Division 1 college sports. The NCAA limits Division 1 women's soccer teams to fourteen scholarships, and the average roster size is thirty-one players. Men's soccer teams have 9.9 scholarships to divide among a typical roster of thirty-two players. Given the vast investment in college football—eighty-five scholarships in a male-only sport are a huge commitment of resources—Title IX-inspired policies aimed at producing gender equity in college athletics means that some women's sports have ratios of roster size to scholarship limit that are more favorable to student athletes than are corresponding men's sports. So, for example, Division 1 women's volleyball rosters average eighteen players and teams have twelve scholarships (while men's volleyball, with a much smaller participant pool, has 4.5 scholarships for Division 1 teams with an average roster of twenty-one players).

Despite the allure of getting a "ride" to college on a full athletic scholarship, most Division 1 athletic scholarships are shared among two or more students and, while valuable, do not constitute the free ride of youth sports lore. In fact, a Division 1 scholarship, even including football and basketball in the calculation, averages about $18,000,[29] less than the cost of tuition at public universities and far below tuition costs at private colleges.

While Division 1 sports get just about all of the public attention—with live televised events, regular coverage by major sports broadcasters and daily newspapers, and significant licensing of team apparel—Division 1 athletes represent a minority of all college athletes. This is little known within youth sports families, and it is not uncommon for aspiring college athletes to equate college sports with Division 1 programs. This can lead parents to make decisions based on a false understanding of the structure of NCAA sports.

Let's recap. The odds of playing collegiate sports are low, fewer than one in ten, and the odds of making a coveted Division 1 roster are even lower, less than one in fifty. What's more, the likelihood a high school athlete will get a college scholarship is about one in 100, and most scholarship recipients outside of the "revenue generating" sports of basketball and football receive partial scholarships rather than "full rides." Finally, the vast majority of young athletes who play college sports do not play in Division 1 but play for programs that are not part of the televised and branded collegiate sports landscape. Overall, more than 80 percent of college athletes play on teams outside of the NCAA's Division 1—in the NCAA's Division 2 or 3, junior college, NAIA or other college sports associations—but they are largely invisible (or mistakenly believed to be Division 1 athletes) within youth sports circles.

The Impact on Public Perception

Given what we know, it is surprising that a narrowly defined dream of playing college sports persists in the minds of parents in such a robust way. The reality of the college sports landscape does little to dampen the hopes and dreams of young athletes and their families seeking recognition, status, scholarship dollars, and four more years of highly competitive sporting activity.

Explaining the persistence of this dream in the face of long odds is no simple task. Part of an explanation would take us deep into the adolescent psyche, where future hopes and dreams are constructed. Adults are often reluctant to crush youthful dreams, and asking young athletes to face up to just how unlikely their dream really is can seem both cruel and unnecessary. And given just how much space celebrity athletes occupy in our mediascape and broader cultural imagination, it is no surprise that kids build and hold on to dreams of sports stardom. At the same time, the perceived benefits of athletic success—public attention, money for college, perhaps even future fame and fortune—are so high many parents are willing to gamble that their child might end up being the rare sports prodigy who makes it.

That this willingness to envision future athletic stardom for a child often persists well past the time when such a future is even remotely possible is testament to just how deep and powerful the fantasy of sports glory is. However, such dreams, whether long shots or entirely fantastical, don't persist in a vacuum. The oxygen that enlivens these dreams, which keeps them circulating within communities of young athletes and their parents, is a rumor mill full of misinformation. Scholarship dreams are nourished by stories of peers who are on the verge of, or already have, "made it"—or so the stories flowing through local youth sports circles declare.

Parents, coaches, travel clubs, and players themselves often participate in seemingly innocuous forms of exaggeration, inflating stories of athletic success and collegiate opportunity. Incomplete, even inaccurate, information is so common that it is difficult to find terrain on which to evaluate any specific story. Tales of athletic achievement—being actively recruited by college coaches, playing on a college team, getting an athletic scholarship—are powerful status markers for everyone involved. Parents are congratulated for supporting their kids, coaches are recognized for successfully developing young athletes, travel clubs claim success in placing a player, and players receive enthusiastic attention (and sometimes envy) from their peers.

Such status accrues in the telling of the tale. It is not subject to any kind of verification. In many cases, players believed to be heavily recruited to play in the NCAA turn out to be receiving lots of mass emails from coaches and paying large sums to attend showcases. Reports of guaranteed roster spots are often little more than invitations to try out. Purported full rides are actually partial scholarships, only guaranteed for one year. Assertions that a graduating senior is going to College X to play Sport Y are frequently stated with enthusiastic certainty, even when a player is hoping just to make the team.

When players head off to college, most locals only keep up with their future playing days through word of mouth. So it is that one parent we know was happy, if a bit uncomfortable, permitting neighbors and friends—and, perhaps most important, the parents of younger aspiring athletes—to believe that her daughter had received a full athletic scholarship when, in fact, there was no scholarship at all. Another parent we followed talked proudly of his son's recruitment to play on a Division 1 team, when, in fact, he arrived as a "walk on" whose time with the team ended less than a week into the preseason.

Overstating a child's athletic success—or letting stand other people's stories that embellish the truth about a child's sports career—is not a major moral blemish. But it is nonetheless consequential. Misleading stories and misinformation about college sports have a powerful impact on the youth sports ecosystem by ramping up expectations, making it all seem not just possible, but perhaps even easy, and giving young athletes inauthentic examples to emulate. Most of all, the widespread circulation of stories that are only partially true is a potent, if generally unrecognized, force in keeping the college sports dream alive.

Rethinking College Sports

For many young athletes, playing collegiate sports may be a reasonable goal, providing motivation, focus, and an anchor to the educational value of sports. Many young athletes who move on to play college sports have positive experiences. But the benefits of playing college sports rarely match the tenets of the college sports dream. The multiple levels at which the college sports dream is misaligned with the realities of college sports—the recruiting process, the likelihood of playing, the availability of scholarships, and what student athletes gain from the experience—point to one of the ways youth sports culture misleads, in potentially damaging ways, players and their parents.

It is possible, however, to develop a more complex conversation within youth sports circles about collegiate sports. That type of discussion can lead to more informed decision-making by families, less desperation and disappointment, and a richer recognition of the possibilities, challenges, and joys of playing in college. To begin, we need to figure out how to talk more honestly about sports. That is no easy task, but youth sports will continue to be a breeding ground for widespread misinformation and irresponsible fantasy reproduction if we do not rethink how we talk about, and think about, college sports.

One starting point is to recognize that most collegiate athletes do not experience the perceived benefits of status and scholarships or stardom and fame. In fact, most collegiate athletes play in obscurity. They dedicate countless hours, year-round, to their sport, but do so with little recognition or tangible rewards. At many college sporting events, and just about all sports contests outside of major Division 1 sports, the fans in attendance consist mostly of family and friends. The economic benefits for the vast number of college athletes who receive little or no scholarship money are generally limited to a free supply of team gear and subsidized or free travel to off-season training or warm climate tournaments. And a tiny fraction of college athletes is on-track to launch successful professional athletic careers.

Acknowledging how the reality of college athletics deviates from the dream is not a form of criticism of college athletics. Instead, recognizing this mismatch may help us to liberate college sports from the limitations of the dream, which hide the less glamorous, but still very real, value of collegiate sports.

Playing college sports, for many athletes, is shaped most fundamentally by one's experience as a member of an often close-knit team. The sheer number of hours collegiate players spend together—training, practicing, preparing, studying, often sharing living spaces—can be a powerful bonding force. What many college athletes find most memorable about their college playing days are the relationships among teammates, the social capital that helps smooth out the challenges of college life and become enduring social connections. Such connections can be just as significant for the many collegiate athletes who are on team rosters, but rarely if ever have the opportunity to play in games, as they are for the top-performing players.

College athletics can also be an important route—indeed, an incentive—to starting and completing higher education. Even for those athletes who were so focused on sports they thought little of academic pursuits, playing in college is part of the larger endeavor of attending college. Players are likely to find their way to new academic interests, pushed along by their coaches, professors, peers, and student affairs staff and move toward completing college. It is clear that sports can bring young people to college, sometimes when little else is drawing them there, and it also can help keep students in college until they graduate.

Finally, playing in college is an extension, even an intensification, of the learning from sports that begins all the way back in early youth sports programs. We will explore this more fully in our concluding chapter, but we note here that college athletics can be a tremendous source of the life lessons that define so much of the youth sports experience. What young people learn from sports—about failure and success, perseverance and competition, talent and inequality, pride and respect—is an everyday part of the collegiate sports experience.

Most aspiring collegiate athletes never play in college. Many others play sparingly or briefly. Even those who experience athletics as a central part of their collegiate experience are likely to face challenging moments of uncertainty about the meaning of their relationship to sports. Sooner or later, most parents, too, will face similar questions about what the college sports dream is all about, for themselves and their child. And rather than think in instrumental terms, we will all think more clearly and helpfully about the meaning of sports in the lives of young athletes if we focus on questions of identity instead of investments. After all, it is the identity of being an athlete, or being a parent of an athlete, that marks the end of a young athlete's playing days as a significant life transition. When that time comes, and it arrives for everyone, and sooner and more abruptly than they expect, most young athletes (and their parents) are ill equipped to reflect on the meaning of sports in their lives.

CHAPTER FIVE

The Mobile Neighborhood
The Culture of Travel Team Parents

....

"Oh, I love it. Not just watching my own daughter. I know
all of these girls. One of them is my best friend's daughter
and I've known them since they were in kindergarten, so
I love watching all of the games . . . It's just fun. In fact,
I hate it when I have to miss a game."

— *Parent of a travel soccer player* —

....

Lily Wilson started playing soccer when she was six. She immediately took to the sport, asking her parents, Stephen and Jennifer, to drive her to practices early or to practice penalty kicks with her in their backyard. But few of her teammates showed as much enthusiasm for the sport as Lily did, and Stephen and Jennifer were not impressed with the quality of coaching she was receiving on her local recreational team. So, four years ago, when Lily was ten years old, the family decided to leave the town team to join the Cougars, a travel club that practices about thirty minutes from their home.

The Cougars play in a more competitive league. They enter tournaments almost every weekend. Although a majority of the girls on the team attend other high schools, Lily sees them more often than many of the kids who live on her street. And they have much in common. Cougars take soccer seriously. At practices, they don't fool around. When a coach tells them to work harder, they immediately put more effort into the exercise; no one complains. Stephen thinks spending so much time with other kids so focused on soccer has helped Lily raise the level of her game a notch or two. This past year, she earned a starting spot on her high school team, which might not have been possible if she had remained in the recreational league, Stephen tells us.

It isn't easy for Stephen and Jennifer to meet all of the demands associated with travel sports. When Lily switched teams, the expenses increased significantly. Stephen and Jennifer knew that would be the case, but they had not anticipated all the extra money they would need to spend—the extra tank of gas that goes into their car each week, the hotel rooms and meals at weekend tournaments, the souvenir t-shirts. The expenses add up quickly. Both Stephen and Jennifer work, but they are not wealthy, and travel team expenses sometimes push them to their financial limit.

Making sure Lily gets to all of her travel team practices and games is also challenging for the Wilson family. When you include driving time, attending a single practice can eat up close to three hours. Shuttling Lily to soccer practices three times a week is difficult. Lily has two siblings and someone has to stay home to watch them. Also, Stephen regularly has to work late and can't make it home in time to drive Lily to practice. It sometimes feels like soccer dominates life in the Wilson home.

Even though Stephen and Jennifer recognize these challenges, they make things work and try to focus on the positive aspects of their travel team experience. When the Wilsons can't carve out the time to drive Lily to practice, they can usually find another parent to take her. The same is true with tournaments. On a number of occasions, another family has chauffeured Lily to an out-of-state tournament and let her stay in their hotel room. Stephen and Jennifer felt completely comfortable entrusting their daughter to other parents on such occasions and have done the same for other girls on the team.

This is because over the past four years, the Wilsons have become quite close with the other parents on the team. At first, relationships developed through the informal conversations they had with other parents on the sidelines of Cougars practices. Those connections became deeper when families started spending weekends together at tournaments. You get to know people quite well holed up together in a Holiday Inn located several hours from home for three days.

Stephen and Jennifer now consider a number of team parents among their closest friends. This was something they didn't expect when Lily began playing soccer. But with each passing year, the amount of time they spent with families in the neighborhood decreased and the hours surrounded by soccer families grew. Now Cougar families regularly get together to socialize, even during the off-season. It seems like every month they do something together that is unrelated to soccer. Last winter, they spent a day snow tubing at a local recreation park. They also organized parents-only parties throughout the year.

Although Stephen and Jennifer complain about all the time they spend supporting Lily's soccer career, they recognize the benefits of those efforts. While the Wilsons often feel tired and overextended, they also experience a strong sense of connection with other sports families. Those feelings of togetherness, of a common purpose, make the sacrifices they make seem worthwhile.

Travel Sports as a Family Commitment

Youth sports are about more than just what happens on the playing field. They are also about more than just the experiences of the kids who play. As many longtime sports parents know, the world of youth sports brings adults together in significant and enduring ways. What's surprising is how little we recognize the parent connections that help sustain youth sports communities. When we look beyond the popular narratives of out-of-control sports parents, we can begin to see why so many adults invest so much time and energy in their kids' sporting activities.

If we are to understand why so many parents give so much of themselves to their kids' sports, we need to move beyond cynical clichés. Rather than shake our head at the parent who sits quietly in the bleachers long after his child's last game has ended or snicker at adults who return to watch a high school team play in the years after their children have graduated, we can learn something about why youth sports matter by looking more carefully at how parents find meaning in their own youth sports involvement.

As the parents we interviewed reflected on travel team activities, they described their children's development as athletes—and also spoke extensively about their relationships with other team parents. Clearly, joining a travel team had affected them on many levels and in ways they had not anticipated. Sports was just one component of the travel team experience for them.

"When someone tries out for the team," a parent explained to us, "it's not just the kid who's trying out—it's the whole family. It's the parents too." We have seen and heard versions of this observation many times. It would seem to apply to almost any sport or youth team. When we played sports as kids, our parents occasionally attended practices and games; they even brought snacks for the team to a game each season. Clearly, parents have long been involved with their children's sports. But this apparent continuity in parental involvement doesn't capture the full story. Today, travel team parents take on responsibilities that far exceed those of the seasonal sport parent. As the youth sports industry has expanded, the expectations for families have become more complex, the demands more extensive.

We discovered that when parents sign up their children for travel sports, few are aware of the impact that decision will have on their own lives. It seemed as though invisible threads connected parents and children, with the actions of one tugging, often imperceptibly, on the other. To fully understand the nature of youth sports, we need to pay close attention to those webs of relationships and influences.

As travel teams have become more serious, the length of their seasons has expanded. Many travel sports are now played virtually year-round. Soccer parents, for example, told us that when their kids first started playing during their elementary school years, they were free to spend most of the summer doing other things, such as going to camp or spending time with relatives. But around middle school, summer breaks seemed to vanish as clubs started playing in elite tournaments in June and July. By the time soccer players entered ninth grade, the only extended break in travel team schedules occurred in the fall—so that players could play on their high school soccer teams. Other sports have similar schedules, typically with more than one "season" each year, along with various off-season clinics, tournaments, and training sessions.

Travel sports also demand more of parents than recreational sports, in part, due to the distances between game sites. In general, the higher the level of play, the greater the distances that separate teams. For example, travel teams composed of nine- and ten-year-olds typically play other clubs in the same or an adjacent county. This makes it possible for a family to drive to an away game, watch the match, and return home—all within three or four hours. In those cases, parents can arrange their schedules to fit travel games and still do other things on the weekend. But more competitive leagues, like premier leagues in soccer and elite volleyball programs, often include teams from multiple states. Attending a single game may eat up most of the day. Baseball and softball travel teams often play double-headers, which means five or six hours of competition packed into a single day.

The teams we followed in the Hudson Valley region of New York participated in tournaments in New Jersey, Maryland, Virginia, and even Florida (Disney Orlando is a prime location for high profile athletic events). When players are in elementary school, tournaments are typically one-day affairs. But showcase events for middle and high school age players frequently last two or three days. This means athletes, and their parent chauffeurs, sometimes miss a day of school or work to attend a tournament. Whether one-day events with a ten-year-old or a three-day weekend with a high school age player, accompanying a child to a travel tournament requires parents to set aside large chunks of time—and money.

Family Commitments and Connections

The intensity of travel sports imposes distinctive demands on players and parents. Those demands create challenges that are more formidable than those typically associated with recreational sports. The time commitment required of participants, over the course of a week as well as a season, can be overwhelming. As Table 1 illustrates, more than half of the parents we surveyed spend at least nine hours a week helping with their child's travel team, with about a third of parents spending twelve or more hours helping out each week. The time commitment for women is even higher, with 59 percent of mothers reporting they spend at least nine hours each week on travel team activities.

Table 1
Weekly Hours with Child's Sports by Parent Gender [N=502]

On average, during the travel sports season,
what is your best estimate of the number of hours you
spend each week on your child's sports activities?

Parent Gender	< 3 Hours	3–6 Hours	6–9 Hours	9–12 Hours	12–15 Hours	> 15 Hours
Male	3.36%	19.75%	28.15%	21.01%	8.82%	18.91%
Female	3.03%	18.56%	23.11%	20.08%	17.05%	18.18%
Total	**3.19%**	**19.12%**	**25.50%**	**20.52%**	**13.15%**	**18.53%**

Our survey data indicate that the vast majority of parents are deeply engaged with their children's travel teams. A total of 83 percent of respondents said they were "very involved" in their child's sports activities while less than 1 percent of parents said they are not involved at all. As Table 2 shows, this high degree of involvement was consistent among parents with children across the full range of ages, from eight to eighteen. Most of the adults we interviewed discussed in great detail the demands associated with travel team life.

Table 2
Parent Involvement with Sports by Child Age [N=518]

How involved would you say you are
in your child's sports activities?

Player Age	Not Involved at All	Somewhat Involved	Very Involved
8 or younger	0	13.79%	86.21%
9	0	15.09%	84.91%
10	0	18.31%	81.69%
11	2.33%	20.93%	76.74%
12	1.82%	14.55%	83.64%
13	0	14.58%	85.42%
14	1.15%	14.94%	83.91%
15	0	19.67%	80.33%
16	0	17.14%	82.86%
17	0	16.67%	83.33%
18	0	0	100%
Total	**0.58%**	**16.22%**	**83.20%**

Joining a travel team also requires families to increase their financial commitments to their children's athletic activities. Playing on a travel team is significantly more expensive than is the case with local recreational sports programs. According to our survey, the annual cost of playing on travel teams ranged from several hundred dollars to $15,000, with most parents reporting somewhere between $1,000 and $3,000.

Clearly, joining a travel team represents a significant commitment on the part of families. How do adults justify the money and time they are required to invest in their children's athletic activities? As would be expected, the most common motivations parents mentioned as they reflected on the reasons for joining travel teams related to their children's athletic pursuits. But framing the travel team experience solely in terms of athletic benefits oversimplifies what is often an extremely complex process. Our interviews with parents suggest that adults may initially decide to join travel teams with their children's future athletic opportunities in mind, but the connections they develop with other parents cement their commitment to the team and keep them coming back season after season. Just as players form relationships that solidify over time, the communities of travel team parents we observed became progressively more concentrated.

We found that relationships among sports parents evolve in stages, in response to changing expectations and demands placed on families. During the early years of a travel team, adults work together to make sure their children make it to practices and games. They also chat regularly during practices and games. These regular, somewhat structured opportunities to socialize, provide parents with opportunities to get to know each other. Interactions among travel team parents were both more regular and enduring than is common with recreational leagues.

Among the teams we studied, during what we term the second stage of parental interactions, the relationships between adults deepened and took on new dimensions when the clubs began to attend tournaments on a regular basis. Weekend tournaments provide highly concentrated opportunities for parents to interact beyond the playing field. During these multiple-day events, relationships among travel team parents often shift from casual interaction to what could be characterized as "deep involvement." At this stage, the extended time parents spend together, often in unfamiliar settings, creates spaces for them to get to know each other more intimately than is true at regular games or practices. As one mother reflected, "We do have some very friendly people on the team and when we go away on tournaments, we always try to eat dinner together, we hang out together, and we have team parties together. To me, that's very important. It's something I care about." Another parent told us that "You get close because you're staying in hotels with them. We go to Long Island, Massachusetts, Pennsylvania, so we're in hotels with them two nights a week. We're with them a lot."

In many cases, the relationships that formed through sports extended beyond the athletic field. Several of the parents we spoke with observed that their closest friends were other travel team mothers and fathers. In some cases, social events organized by the team represented parents' most consistent opportunities to interact with other adults. One group of travel team parents we followed celebrated New Year's Eve together each year. In other cases, subgroups of parents got together regularly for dinners or special events. Not all parents chose to participate in social activities, but they were constantly available to those who were interested.

Although it may seem natural that a group of adults who spend significant time together will develop a sense of camaraderie, we were surprised by the intensity of some of those relationships. We discovered the travel team community served as a sort of social anchor for many parents. Those adults relied on each other regularly to manage schedules and rides, spent weekends away from home together, and provided each other with emotional support, sometimes over the course of many years.

Many of the people we spoke with described their team as a large extended family; this came up repeatedly in our interviews. Our years of experience as sports parents and coaches only confirms just how frequently sports parents employ the extended family metaphor. The metaphor of travel teams as extended families is not just a cliché. Parents who attend practices and games do more than cheer for their kids. The youth sports sideline often has the feel of a gathering of family or close friends, sharing something they all value and talking about much more than the action on the field or court.

One parent we interviewed described how close she is with other team parents:

Q: How would you describe your relationship with other parents on the team?

A: Um, my best friends are [team] moms. And the rest of the moms, there's at least a half dozen of them, that if I was stuck for a ride for my son or someone to take him for the weekend, I wouldn't even flinch to trust or call or text or ask them can you pick up my son or ask to take him for the weekend. And I would do the same for them. They're great; they're good people.

Q: Do parents get together outside of soccer or activities out of the tournaments organized?

A: The two moms that I'm very close to, we three families make sixteen or seventeen, all of us together. We celebrate Christmas together every year. We do each other's birthdays. We call each other our extended families. Our kids call each other's grandparents Nana, Poppy, and Grandpa. We're very close.

Q: Were you tight with those three families before you joined the team?

A: Didn't know them before.

Adults frequently complained about the responsibilities associated with travel team life. Some seemed overwhelmed by the demanding schedules and high costs. But most of the parents we interviewed emphasized the positive aspects of their bonds with other members of the group. One mother remarked that during the high school sports season, when travel team players play on competing high school teams, "we separate, but then we come home." Some parents remain connected to other team parents even after their children leave a team or stop playing all together, as we discuss in Chapter Nine. When asked if he missed anything about the team his child had recently left, one father replied, "I miss the parents. Like I said, they're a lot of fun. And I mean, it's not like I don't see them. I still email them, and I'm on the email chains that [the coach] sends out."

Replacing the Neighborhood

The sense of community that commonly develops among sports team parents grows from the long hours they spend together. But that time together does not fully explain the reasons so many parents feel such strong connections to their kids' sports teams. Our research suggests that membership in the youth sports community meets a variety of adult needs, some that relate to sports and others that are only indirectly linked to athletics. When we look carefully at interactions among youth sports parents, we not only learn something valuable about the evolution of youth sports in the United States; we also gain fresh insight into ongoing changes in US society.

As we all know from personal experience, the nature of community life has changed significantly over the past fifty years. Adults as well as children organize their daily lives to fit a different set of conditions than was the case a generation ago. Economic, social, and technological advances have combined to reconfigure the way we interact with one another. Our lives no longer resemble scenes from *Leave It to Beaver* or *The Brady Bunch*. In the past, families living in the same neighborhood tended to form networks centered on children and family life. Parents could depend on other adults on the street to look after their children, and neighbors constituted a valued support system. Families living in close proximity to one another also socialized together, formally and informally. Teenagers babysat younger children who lived nearby. Community life was localized and predictable. One of the coaches we spoke with reflected on such changes:

> Unfortunately, I think the whole fabric of our society is changing. When I grew up, on Sunday you went to church. And you were at your hometown and your community. And I think more and more people are traveling on the weekends, and I don't know if that's a good thing for our society, but that's where you're going to make your friends and you'll be away at tournaments three or four times a year for several days. I think it's changing a lot.

Although this coach's observations were based on his own experiences, substantial research supports his view of the world. Over the past two decades, sociologists have been studying the changing role of neighborhoods in American society. They have carefully analyzed the factors that are reshaping social life and the ways that citizens are responding to those changes. Although none of these studies focus on youth sports, their findings help explain how and why so many adults find meaningful social connections through their kids' sports teams.

One of the most influential books that explored this topic, *Bowling Alone,* by Robert Putnam, documents the gradual loosening of connections that historically formed the bedrock of neighborhood life in America. Putnam observes that since the 1950s, Americans have become increasingly disconnected from family, friends, and neighbors. As social relationships have loosened, we are spending more time by ourselves, engaged in individualized activities. Theda Skocpol followed up Putnam's research and drew similar conclusions. In her book, *Diminished Democracy,* Skocpol concludes that people today are likely to join groups that require fewer responsibilities of their members who interact at more superficial levels.

It appears that connections among neighbors have become increasingly fragile. For example, in 2005, almost half (47 percent) of Americans indicated that they knew "none, almost none, or a few" of their neighbors by name. And the percentage of US citizens who reported that they never socialized with a neighbor increased from 20 percent to 30 percent between the mid-1970s and the 2000s. As Marc J. Dunkelman observes in his book, *The Vanishing Neighbor,* "Today, being 'neighborly' means leaving those around you in peace."

As neighborhoods have ceased to create a form of social glue, technology has filled this gap for many people. More and more, we interact via email and text message and on social media, often at the expense of face-to-face interactions. Dunkelman notes that technology makes it "incredibly easy to maintain one-dimensional friendships." On one hand, it has become easier to forge connections with strangers than with people who live down the street. Clicking the "like" button on Facebook or following someone with similar interests on X (formerly Twitter) requires less effort than establishing an ongoing relationship with a neighbor. Electronic relationships, however, can be superficial and undependable. Unfriending someone on Facebook is just as easy as friending them. An electronic community can cease to function with one pull of a plug.

Although youth sports parents regularly use various social media to communicate—many teams have social media accounts or use a youth sports league app for schedule updates and photo sharing—they also value the kind of personal connections with other adults that sports can provide. For many, chatting with other parents at practices, games, and tournaments offers the most regular opportunities to socialize with friends. Some adults interact with other travel team parents more often than they do with people who live in their neighborhoods. In a sense, travel team communities have become "mobile neighborhoods" that provide dependable social connections for parents who may not socialize with the people who live near them on a regular basis.

As they chat during games and practices, parents discuss the latest team developments and upcoming events on the team schedule. But many also spend a significant amount of time sharing information about things unrelated to sports. For example, at one practice we attended, parents formed clusters on the side of the field. A few wore shirts and hoodies emblazoned with the team logo, making their connections to the group obvious. Most paid little attention to the action on the field. Instead, they were chatting about a recent power outage in town, an ill relative, customs in their home countries, and car problems. One dad passed around his cell phone, sharing a picture of his daughter. At weekend baseball doubleheaders, parents often sat on folding chairs lined up along the fence, shifting over the course of the day to talk with each other in small groups. The conversations ranged from shared rides home and upcoming college visits to family health issues and summer jobs. In subsequent weekends, the conversations seemed to pick up without missing a beat. Similarly, at the championship game of a statewide soccer tournament, parents moved seamlessly back-and-forth between commentary about on-field action and talk about each other's work lives and upcoming travel plans.

These rather informal but regular gatherings provide parents with opportunities to talk about whatever is on their minds. The content of conversation seems less important than the fact that people are meeting face-to-face with people they know, who listen to them, and who they can expect to see again on the sidelines next week. When a mother or father talks about something they care about, they receive more than an emoji in response. They don't have to worry about whether or not a comment they make will earn a "like" from followers. And while this same informal interaction takes place at local recreational sports events, travel team communities are more intense. The mobile neighborhood of the travel sports team offers many parents enduring friendships and connections they find gratifying.

Insiders and Outsiders

The intensity of interaction that is common among travel sports parents isn't for everyone. While some adults derive great satisfaction from the close-knit travel team community, others feel more conflicted about the situation. Most parents we interviewed spoke with enthusiasm about the relationships they had formed with other travel team families. However, just as with groups of adolescents, parent communities can be hierarchical. Not all adults view themselves as equal participants within those communities. When we spoke with parents, "insiders" tended to speak glowingly about team activities, while "outsiders" expressed more ambiguous feelings about the group.

In contrast to youth cultures, a parent's location in the hierarchy of social relations seemed to be largely self-selected. Some parents were enthusiastic all-in participants, even if they hadn't expected to become so involved. Adults who chose not to organize their social lives around the travel team, on the other hand, sometimes felt disconnected from the team community. One couple we spoke with described themselves as "peripheral" members of the parent group and told us they had cordial but not close connections with the parents they referred to as "the inner circle."

Individuals who self-identified as occupying the "secondary circle" of parents may have felt distanced from the core group of team parents, but they also recognized the benefits of being surrounded by a highly committed group of parents. In some ways, that made it harder for parents to say anything negative about the parent community. For example, one parent told us: "I feel like I can call on them for things and they're very nice people. They're wonderful people. They would do anything. But" she continued, "I don't have the same, I don't know, intensity that they do about the game. . . . I probably don't share the same enthusiasm about traveling to tournaments that they do. . . . I think it's wonderful that these parents want to do that, but it's not so easy for me. Sometimes I feel bad about that. I feel guilty because I'm not the same as the other parents."

Several people we spoke with expressed similar sentiments. The powerful ties that developed among travel team parents created a sense of belonging for some adults; for others, the strength of the parent community raised all sorts of questions about the role of youth sports in the lives of their children. For such parents, travel teams already ate up a significant portion of their personal and family time. They were not interested in the commitment of time and emotion involved with joining a mobile neighborhood of the youth sports parent community. From their perspective, attending social events with other team parents was another example of the over-the-top nature of travel sports.

Filling a Void

For a variety of reasons—safety, scheduling, work commitments, family structure—adults now look beyond the boundaries of their neighborhoods for social support. In today's fluid, fast-paced society, people form communities that are not bound by geography. Instead, they increasingly forge relationships with others whose social worlds look more like their own. This leads many to develop connections with like-minded individuals online or in locations far from their homes. Parents, in particular, seek out supportive relationships with others who understand the everyday challenges they face.

Psychologists Emily A. Greenfield and Laurent Reyes have found that "supportive neighbor relationships are especially important for the positive and more developmental and functional aspects of mental health," and adults who interact regularly with neighbors report higher levels of psychological well-being. For increasingly large numbers of adults, however, opportunities to connect with neighbors are infrequent. This helps to explain why parents develop such strong attachments to their children's travel teams.

The intensity of travel sports imposes distinctive demands on players and parents; those demands create challenges that are more formidable than those typically associated with recreational sports. The time commitment required of participants, over the course of a week as well as a season, can be overwhelming. Despite such demands, we found that most parents are deeply engaged with their children's travel teams. For many parents, what motivates their continuing involvement in travel sports is far more than a commitment to their children. Instead, parent involvement in travel sports is sustained by the development of social connections among team parents.

In multiple settings, but particularly at day- or weekend-long travel tournaments, we observed travel team parents talking with each other about family, work, school, vacation plans, and other topics connected with their everyday life. Through those activities, they developed relationships that anchored their social lives. Other travel team parents became their most trusted allies. In times of need, they were the people they turned to for support. As the demands placed on families become more extensive, relationships among adults tend to become more complex and enduring. Over time, parents come to value the social aspects of travel team communities, and the emotional support they derived from other parents. A family who joins a travel team may remain a member of that community for a decade or more. Over that period of time, parents often develop long-standing relationships with other members of their mobile neighborhood.

In this way, youth sports communities fill a void that is emerging in the lives of many adults. In a society where community ties have steadily loosened, the activities connected with youth sports can offer a predictable regularity. Parents like Stephen and Jennifer may initially sign up their children to play sports without giving the idea a great deal of thought. Often, they are simply looking for ways to keep their children active and to help them make friends. Gradually, though, they come to value the social aspects of travel team communities and the emotional support they derive from other parents. In this way, travel team communities enrich the social worlds of parents who are trying to create positive experiences both for their children and, indirectly, for themselves.

CHAPTER SIX

Not Always on Their Best Behavior

Parents On and Off the Sidelines

....

"I hate to say it but I was almost thinking about dealing with the parents more than even the kids, you know what I mean? . . . Because once you bring in parents that are difficult, the whole experience becomes painful, you know what I mean."

— *Youth sports coach* —

....

Passionately devoted to his son's soccer career, Larry Millikson rarely misses a practice or game. Although he was a capable high school player, Larry never earned any awards or received any special recognition. His son, Keith, on the other hand, has excelled on the soccer pitch since he started playing at age five. Most kids don't sign up for travel teams until they are nine or ten, but Keith played up a year and earned a spot on a travel team when he was only eight. Even though he is younger than most of his teammates, Keith plays in the starting line-up and is one of the leading scorers on his club. Larry has big dreams for his son and is willing to do just about whatever it will take to help him succeed.

Other parents on the team are quite aware of Larry's commitment to his son's athletic career. They have become acclimated to his constant shouting during practices and games.

These diatribes are sometimes directed at referees and opposing players, but, more often, Larry focuses his comments on Keith. Throughout games, he patrols the sidelines exhorting his son to work harder or make smarter decisions but also applauding noteworthy plays. Keith rarely acknowledges his father's presence.

Although parents frequently comment on Larry's antics among themselves, they are not so bold as to tell him that they find his behavior problematic. Clearly, Larry's actions make other parents uncomfortable but saying that directly to him would cross an invisible line. The only person who ever tells Larry he needs to tone it down is his wife, but her words rarely have any impact on his actions.

This situation is complicated by the fact that Larry never hits his son or acts in a way that is unequivocally abusive. The stream of remarks directed at his son is annoying to others, but not usually offensive. They tend to generate rolled eyes rather than outrage. Complicating the situation is the fact that Keith is a very good soccer player. Larry may approach his role as the parent of an athlete a bit too seriously, but is it possible that his son has risen to the top as a result of Larry's single-minded devotion to soccer? Does Keith's success justify his father's behavior? These questions are never discussed by other parents, but they seem to be on the minds of many.

So Larry continues to make his presence known at most soccer events, while other parents tolerate behavior they find inappropriate. Members of the team family shake their heads, but avoid addressing the issue directly, and a delicate sense of harmony is preserved.

In the previous chapter, we explored the relationships that develop between parents associated with travel teams. Our analysis focused on the factors that reinforce adults' commitments to those clubs and the benefits they derive from investing so much time in their children's athletic activities. In this chapter, we look at parent conduct from a different perspective: how their behavior at public events affects others. Why do people like Larry Millikson display such passion at their children's games? Media reports on youth sports often highlight characters like Larry, holding them up as examples of what is wrong with a system that has run off the rails. But does he represent the typical sports parent, or is he an outlier?

During the time we spent studying youth sports, we paid close attention to the behavior of parents. Eager to better understand the role adults play in their children's athletic careers, we took extensive notes at practices, games, and tournaments, and asked parents to share their thoughts about their goals for their sons and daughters. Clearly, the growth of the travel team industry has raised the stakes for young athletes as well as their parents. How are parents responding to that pressure?

Behavior on the Field

Analyzing the observation notes and interview transcripts we collected revealed some interesting patterns in their behavior. The adults we observed fell into three broad groups: calmly supportive, enthusiastically engaged, and line crossers.

Calmly Supportive Parents (CSP)

When reflecting on your own experiences as an athlete or the teams your child played for, you might have trouble coming up with parents who fit in this category because they do not usually attract a great deal of attention. These parents regularly attend practices and games but rarely make a lot of noise. Some of them sit among more vociferous parents while others find spots away from the center of action. CSPs are careful not to do anything that might detract from their children's accomplishments.

Outsiders might assume these parents are less interested in the action on the field than other fans, but our interviews suggest otherwise. CSPs are just as invested in their children's athletic performance as other adults—they just do not feel the need to express that support as overtly as others. Rather than scream out when a play excited or upset them, they are likely to clap or nod. They don't stand out.

Some CSPs do not display their emotions more openly due to their limited knowledge of the sport. Because they did not play the sport at a high level, they may not feel qualified to express their emotions forcefully in public. For others, unobtrusively observing an athletic competition fits with their character. These people feel more comfortable letting others dominate social interactions. And, finally, some parents consciously choose not to yell or scream as a sort of critique of other adults who, in their opinion, behave inappropriately. In certain situations, CSPs may become so excited by action on the court or field that they join the more vocal parents, but such outbursts are rare.

Enthusiastically Engaged Parents (EEP)

As we have noted, participating in travel sports requires families to invest more time, money, and effort than is true of local leagues that play for a single season that lasts only a few months. The intensity of the travel team experience tends to heighten parents' interest in sports activities. Surrounded by other families equally engaged in on-the-field action, they form an animated rooting section. These parents do not hesitate to express their feelings about what they see. They cheer boisterously when an athlete makes an outstanding play or their team scores a run. When a referee or umpire makes a call they do not agree with, EEPs often erupt in catcalls. Fouls made by opposing players can also elicit strong responses from these parents.

The percentage of EEPs seems to increase as their children get older. Some mothers and fathers who start out calmly supportive gradually morph into EEPs. Over time, they become more invested in sporting activities that may not have initially attracted their interest. As the stakes rise, so does their emotional investment in their children's athletic success. Interestingly, this group includes roughly equal numbers of men and women. We had expected that fathers would display more enthusiasm for sporting events than their spouses, but this did not prove to be the case. Adults of both genders enjoy throwing themselves into athletic contests and expressing their opinions with gusto.

Although EEPs occasionally let their emotions override common sense, they are usually careful not to lose control. They have a sense of what types of behavior are viewed as unacceptable and try not to cross into that territory. At times they become quite vocal, but rarely do they use offensive language or viciously attack others. In other words, they behave like adults—energetic and demonstrative adults who understand that extreme behavior might embarrass themselves and their children.

Line Crossers (LC)

Not all parents have the tools required to regulate their own behavior. Some let the intensity of youth sports get the best of them. They are so committed to making sure their sons and daughters reach the upper echelons of their sport that they frequently lose their sense of perspective. These are the mothers and fathers who scream obscenities at opposing players, heckle referees, and publicly berate their children when they make mistakes. Like Larry Millikson, the father profiled at the beginning of this chapter, Line Crossers believe their faith in their child's athletic potential justifies the things they do and say. In contrast to EEPs, who usually self-correct after they act inappropriately, LCs rarely display any inclination to modify their behavior. They lack self-awareness.

Parents who fall in this group tend not to view their behavior as outside the norm. Instead, they see themselves as strong allies and advocates for their children. This helps to explain why they may seem unaware of the effect they have on other parents. Their narrow focus on their children's athletic careers often blinds them to the repercussions of their own words and actions. A conviction that they are acting in the interests of their children helps them rationalize behavior that others may find problematic. During important games, they develop a sort of tunnel vision that blinds them to what is going on around them. All that matters is how their child is performing in that moment.

LCs are ubiquitous, but relatively small in number. They take up space—physically, aurally, and mentally. We remember them because they do outrageous things. After a game ends, we are more likely to recall the parent who screamed at his daughter than those who sat quietly in the stands. At the games and tournaments we attended, we usually spotted a few LCs among each group of parents. They sometimes made comments that would not be tolerated in other public spaces. Those instances are firmly etched in our memories, even though they were outside the norm.

We came up with these categories after completing our research and studying our observation notes and interview transcripts. We did not categorize parents as we attended practices or games. For this reason, it is not possible to offer any statistics about the exact number of adults who fell into each category. The vast majority of parents we studied, however, fit into the group we label Enthusiastically Engaged parents. A much smaller number of adults—perhaps 15–20 percent—displayed the characteristics of Calmly Supportive Parents. Finally, as noted above, a couple of parents on each of the teams we observed qualified as regular Line Crossers.

It is important to note that these categories are fluid. We offer them to highlight the range of attitudes and behavior of the parents we observed. Individuals who generally fit one category sometimes displayed characteristics of another. This was especially true of EEPs, who sometimes let their emotions get the best of them. During heated contests, they could turn into Line Crossers, yelling at umpires or publicly criticizing their own children. After things calmed down, however, they reverted to previous patterns of conduct. In contrast with persistent LCs, they were usually aware when they acted inappropriately and made efforts to regain their composure.

Explanations for Parent Behavior

The information provided above indicates that most parents who attend youth sporting events understand what is expected of them and try to behave appropriately. They may, at times, do things they later regret, but such digressions represent the exception rather than the norm. At most athletic contests we observed, parents eagerly supported their children from the sidelines or stands. They cheered when their team scored a run or a basket and offered words of encouragement when things did not go their way.

We do not want to downplay, however, the influence of the Line Crossers. Though small in number, their behavior had an outsized influence on other spectators. When one parent shouted out an obscenity or inappropriate comment, it registered with everyone sitting nearby. In many cases, other parents communicated their disapproval of Line Crossers through eye rolls, whispered comments, and movement to other spots in the stands. Fans were often embarrassed by the actions of LCs. The outrageous actions of one parent could negatively affect the reputation of the entire team.

Adults are keenly aware of LCs. Parents, coaches, and referees all expressed criticism of fans who could not control their emotions. Nevertheless, they almost never shared their displeasure directly with the person who was ruffling feathers. There seems to be an unspoken code among the parents that criticizing a member of one's family is acceptable, but expressing disapproval of players or parents who are not relatives is not. This carefully choreographed system of avoiding conflict reminded us of the ways alcoholism is often addressed in our society. Friends of alcoholics recognize the symptoms of the disease yet refrain from discussing the topic with the person suffering. In avoiding the situation, they can enable the problematic behavior.

Youth sports culture publicly decries parents who act inappropriately yet tacitly accepts that conduct. The system has done a much better job educating and reforming the actions of coaches. The leagues we studied generally require coaches to attend training seminars that we found informative and useful. Many have also instituted systems for coaches to monitor their peers. For example, they may be required to rate the behavior of other teams and coaches after games and submit those evaluations to league administrators. Teams that consistently earn high marks receive awards for good sportsmanship.

The only formal tool we came across that encourages parents to think seriously about their actions is the Code of Conduct parents are often required to sign at the beginning of a season. But very few of the adults we spoke with could recall the contents of that document. Most Codes of Conduct do include plans for responding to parents who do not follow through on their pledges to display good sportsmanship. For example, one such code we studied states that "If I fail to abide by the aforementioned rules and guidelines, I will be subject to disciplinary action that could include, but is not limited to the following:

- Verbal warning by official, head coach, and/or member of league organization

- Written warning

- Parental game suspension with written documentation of incident

- Parental season suspension

On the surface, this seems like an appropriate plan for responding to parents who violate behavioral norms. It articulates a clear set of consequences that escalate in severity over time. If applied consistently, the Code of Conduct could reduce or eliminate unacceptable activity on the sidelines. Yet in our experience, Codes of Conduct are rarely taken seriously. They provide coaches, referees, and league officials with the authority to respond to unruly parents, but over the two years we conducted this study, we only witnessed one referee who did so. At that soccer match, a group of parents who had been vociferously complaining about calls they didn't agree with was instructed to move to a location 100 feet away from the playing field before the game resumed. Coaches also have the authority to reprimand unruly parents, but we never saw this happen.

The reality is that coaches and umpires are too focused on what is happening on the field to closely monitor the behavior of parents. As a result, parents are generally left to monitor their own behavior. Most of them do a fairly good job at this. They cheer their team on and refrain from doing anything to embarrass themselves or their children. At many athletic competitions, though, the excitement level gradually escalates, leading some adults to lose their composure. Caught up in this fervor, EEPs transform into Line Crossers. Individuals who might normally catch themselves before doing something they might regret feel emboldened to express their feelings at the top of their lungs. The fact that they are not acting alone seems to provide a sort of justification for such behavior. The power of the group overrides individual judgment.

In most cases, parents direct their ire at referees, raising questions about officials' eyesight, impartiality, or judgment. Rarely did we observe parents use profanity. Rather, it was the volume and intensity of their harangues that made such tirades so impactful. Most officials seemed to have developed very thick skins. Some gave groups of Line Crossing parents disapproving looks, but they rarely said anything. It appears that referees and umpires have come to accept unruly behavior from parents as an unavoidable part of the game. Cognizant that their actions will not be punished, parents continue to erupt during key flashpoints in games. After a few minutes, they usually cool down and show a greater sense of decorum. But there is always a chance they will transform back into Line Crossers at some point.

Behavior Off the Field

Disorderly behavior at competitions tends to attract the most attention from the media. Images of parents storming on a field to challenge an umpire or breaking into fights in the stands make good click bait. Newspapers, Facebook pages, and TikTok videos all provoke viewers with portraits of Line Crossers. Although we do find such behavior problematic, as we note above, it is not as common as one might think. It is important to address adults who create disturbances at athletic events. Kids should not have to worry about the possibility that one of their parents will act inappropriately. That has been the case for decades. Our research, however, draws attention to an issue that has become more salient in recent years: parents who put excessive pressure on their children to perform. In a system that often emphasizes products over process, many parents make demands of their children that impede their physical, emotional, and physical development.

When we asked people to reflect on the actions of sports parents that concerned them, they rarely described outbursts they had witnessed on athletic fields. They were much more likely to share their concerns about the pressure some people put on their children. Parents acknowledged that children benefited from participating in high level competition, but also indicated that excessive pressure can be destructive. They talked extensively about adults they knew who placed what they considered an unhealthy emphasis on their kids' athletic performance. It wasn't individual outbursts that concerned them as much as persistent pressure to meet their expectations. Especially concerning to the people we interviewed were parents who let their own aspirations override what was best for their children.

In a commercialized, profit-driven system, it is easy to let success on the field take precedence over other factors. As one mother observed, "There wasn't so much pressure placed on kids when I was growing up. Now, kids feel the weight of the world is on their shoulders. If they don't live up to everyone's expectations, they feel like they have failed." In many cases, it is the parents who generate that pressure. Another person related that "A lot of our friends are really intense. That makes it hard for us to hang out with them. We're so different. It's crazy how hard parents push their kids. And I don't think it's the coaches who create the pressure. It's the parents."

Resisting pressure to succumb to that pressure, however, can be an ongoing challenge, as the following exchange between two parents illustrates:

Father: I think there's a problem and we're all part of the problem. We're all paying the fees and driving kids to these tournaments and worrying about winning games. We all have the right intentions, but we don't always follow through on them.

Mother: I disagree. I don't think we all have the best intentions. I think a lot of parents want their kids to become professional athletes. It's disgusting. When I see what my kid is going through, it makes me worry.

Some parents find a way to maintain a sense of perspective, to focus on the developmental needs of their kids. Quite often, though, the desire to set up their children for success clouds their judgment. According to one mother, "It is an overly competitive—a toxic environment that is not what is best for kids. If you try to make up for your own weaknesses by pushing your kids, how is that going to help them? But I think a lot of parents do that without even realizing it." Similar to the Line Crossers described above, parents who are narrowly focused on advancing their children's athletic careers tend to lack self-awareness. They can unknowingly engender a debilitating fear of failure in their children.

This situation reveals an additional layer of the concept of the mobile community we discuss in Chapter Five. As we observed, travel team communities help parents develop a sense of belonging within a society that has become increasingly divided. Parents value those connections. However, becoming attached to a community of likeminded people can also make it difficult for individuals to objectively see the impact of the decisions they make. The mobile community can serve as a social safety net, but it can also create a sort of echo chamber. Parents who are constantly surrounded by peers who have all centered their lives on their children's athletic lives are unlikely to call attention to express concerns about the pressure other members of that community place on their kids to excel athletically.

Final Thoughts

As youth sports have become more serious and competitive, the stakes have increased for most participants. This has heightened the pressures experienced by parents who have lofty expectations for their sons and daughters. It is not surprising that in this environment, adults sometimes lose their composure. When someone is convinced his child is destined for great things, anything that threatens to interfere with that trajectory can seem momentous. Although most of the parents we observed usually displayed good sportsmanship from the stands, they occasionally let their emotions get the best of them. And that boisterousness often spreads among fans, creating a snowballing effect that was difficult to stop.

When is boisterous cheering admirable and when does it become a problem? What specific behavior from fans is appropriate and what is unacceptable? These are difficult questions to answer. Most of us would agree with broad statements included in sports Codes of Conduct for parents. For example, the Little League Sport Parent Code of Conduct is anchored by six core principles:

- Trustworthiness
- Respect
- Responsibility
- Fairness
- Caring
- Good Citizenship

But what do these ideals look like in practice, and how do we know when they have been violated? Even more specific statements from Codes of Conduct that we came across, such as "I will be a positive role model and encourage sportsmanship by showing respect and courtesy," may be interpreted differently by different people. And some seem almost impossible to enforce, such as "I will teach my child to play by the rules and to resolve conflicts in a sportsmanlike manner."

We would probably all agree that if an adult hit a player, that would be unacceptable and warrant a strong response from an official or league. But what about a parent who incessantly yells at her daughter to try harder? What should be done when a child appears to be experiencing extreme stress as a result of parental pressure? Is Larry Millikson doing his son a favor by pushing him so hard, or will his approach have negative consequences in the long run?

These questions highlight the nebulous, often conflicting, contours of the space parents occupy in the contemporary world of youth sports. That world is characterized by a set of broad ideals about how adults can support the development of young players. Those ideals, however, are rarely supported by clearly articulated and consistently implemented procedures related to parent conduct. This situation mirrors broader tensions related to youth sports that pervade our society. We espouse ideas like fair play, sportsmanship, balance between sports and academics, development over winning, and teamwork, yet also celebrate individuals who are willing to do whatever it takes to defeat their opponents. Troubling behavior, by players as well as their parents, is frequently overlooked when athletes excel on the playing field. We seem to hold outstanding athletes to a different set of standards than their less accomplished peers; the same is true of the mothers and fathers who nurture their careers.

Although these tensions have always plagued youth sports, the gradual shift from community-based athletics to more elite travel team play has exacerbated these conflicts. The stakes have become higher for everyone involved. It was easier to maintain a sense of perspective and balance when Little League was the most popular organized sporting organization in the country. Participants were likely to have established relationships with players on opposing teams, seasons were shorter, and the connections to future athletic opportunities less salient. The creation and expansion of elite leagues that demand greater investments from participants and entice them with potential opportunities to earn college athletic scholarships at some point in the future has created the impetus for more extreme behavior.

The economic realities of travel sports add fuel to that fire. It should not surprise us that parents who begin investing significant amounts of time and money in their children's athletic careers when they are young doggedly support their children and sometimes lose their sense of perspective. Teams that depend on the monthly fees they collect from families may hesitate to clamp down on questionable behavior from parents, especially if their children excel on the playing field. Upsetting parents, even if they violate club rules, could undercut their profits. This reality reduces pressure to enforce a set of behavioral consequences for parents. As a result, parents are frequently left to police themselves. Most parents do a good job monitoring their own behavior, but they sometimes cross lines. The lack of clearly articulated and consistently enforced policies can create combustible settings that bring out the worst in people. Extreme behavior is looked down upon but tolerated. Given these realities, it is not surprising that people like Larry Millikson continue to patrol the sidelines season after season, screaming at their children, opposing players, and referees.

CHAPTER SEVEN

Exceptional . . . or Not
The Politics of Youth Sports

*"It's interesting how basically egos get involved and parents
who are influential can control a team. And I can tell you,
I know firsthand, there are parents that help dictate the
direction of a team and who makes a team."*

— *Father of a high school athlete* —

One idea that came up frequently in the conversations we had with parents related to the power certain adults acquired and how they used that power. As one mother observed, "Sports is so political now." When asked to clarify what she meant, the parent responded, "Parents have such an influence over kids' sports. They have an influence on everything. For example, they influence what teams their kids are placed on. They try to get involved in the administrative side and try to get their kids on certain teams." This wasn't a topic we expected to hear so much about, but it was clearly on parents' minds.

Parents are highly sensitive to issues of fairness in their children's lives. They may not say anything when their daughter does not earn a spot on a particular team or their son doesn't get the playing time his performance would merit—but they notice those things. Over time, they become sensitive to questionable behavior by coaches, board members, and other parents. Some people choose to overlook adults who use their power to create advantages for their children. One mother, for instance, related that "I was less informed because I chose to be. I wasn't involved in the politics of the league, and I never will be. So my kids didn't get the same opportunities as some of the other kids. I think we're a little more chill than most parents." Other parents were disturbed by evidence of adults wielding power to create advantages for their children. Some voiced their concerns to coaches and board members. Most remained silent, convinced that complaining would not have any effect.

In this chapter we provide an overview of the levers of power in youth sports today. We draw primarily from the observations shared with us by parents who had a lot to say about this topic. They eagerly reflected on the ways politics influence the process of selecting players to play on teams, decisions about who plays what position and when, and the treatment of young athletes. We learned that when parents feel obligated to negotiate a political system with unclear rules, they are more likely to splurge on the most expensive equipment, enroll their children in private training sessions, and lose sight of why they initially signed up their children to play organized sports.

Factor 1: Forming Teams

In most recreational leagues, every child who signs up to play is placed on a team. In some cases, the league randomly assigns players to teams. Another common approach is for coaches to select their players through a sort of round-robin draft. Once the season starts, everyone is also guaranteed a certain amount of playing time, regardless of ability level.

That is not the case for many youth sports leagues today. As the emphasis has shifted from development to performance, the stakes have escalated. Travel teams and academies usually require potential players to take part in a series of high stakes try outs. At those sessions, coaches or league officials roam the field, clipboards in hand, rating the participants. The purpose of the auditions is not to allocate players to teams in the hopes of achieving some sort of competitive balance, but to determine who can join the club and who will be rejected. It is important to recognize that in many settings, the athletes being judged are eight or nine years old. They may not be prepared to make sense of what they have been through or why they are not selected to play for a particular team.

Some of the parents we interviewed thought that this approach was a reasonable way of ensuring that teams attracted the most talented players. From their perspective, creating teams that include individuals of varying athletic abilities is a disservice to players with more advanced skills. One father explained to us that his son "moved to the travel team when he was eleven because his team wasn't as competitive as the other team, and we wanted to take the next step with him. With the rec team, half the time they didn't have a full team because people were at basketball or baseball. The next step, if you're serious, is to keep moving, taking the next step." Another father commented, "I think travel more than anything is—we're playing baseball. This is about baseball. This is not Little League. It's not, go have fun with our buddies and goof around. It's baseball." These men, like several of the parents we interviewed, viewed the switch from recreational to travel leagues as a logical progression. Playing for a more competitive team was a necessity if their children were going to keep developing as athletes. In a hierarchical system, separating serious athletes from kids who want to "goof around" makes sense.

Although adults tended to understand the reasons for holding try outs and rejecting some applicants, many of the parents we spoke with expressed the concerns about the selection process. Parents usually had limited knowledge about that process, which could breed skepticism and distrust. A common criticism shared with us was that when it comes to trying out for travel teams, not everyone is given an equal shot; decisions about who makes a team and who is cut are not always based on an athlete's abilities or performance. Parents frequently raised questions about coaches' motives for inviting certain players to join their teams, as the following statements illustrate:

> We had try outs for an elite team and several players didn't get picked. But then we found out that after the regular try outs they didn't have enough players to form a team, so the coach called some families who didn't go to the try outs. He offered to have private try outs for them, and they were picked for the team. He invited these kids to play on the team, but if they don't play well, the coach will drop them quicker than shit and get other kids to play on the team.

> The day they called players to let them know what team they would be on, my daughter was really excited. She thought she would make the A team. But then she didn't get a call all day. Finally, she learned that she had been placed on the C team. She was devastated. "What did I do wrong? What did I do to make this happen?" She cried her eyes out that night. It was terrible, for her and for us. The coach had told her what a great athlete she was, but then didn't move her up. I didn't know what was going on so I talked to a parent who is more involved in the league. She told me how the league works and how they decide on teams. She said that it is mostly based on what a few parents want to happen.

> There were instances where I've seen coaches choose one kid over another because the parents were either very good friends with him or would do other favors for him on the side. Stuff like that would basically sway their decisions. And you know, you get favors paid, since the dads are friends. One of the dads is a coach or an assistant coach on a team. He says, "I think Bobby should really be on the team, even though he didn't have a great try out. Let's just get Bobby on that team." That stuff happens. You hear what's going on.

We recognize that many youth sports teams are not plagued by these issues. In cities across the country, coaches make decisions about who to include on their rosters based on their honest assessments of potential players. However, in the interviews we conducted with parents, concerns about the conduct of coaches and league officials were raised frequently. The volume of those critical comments suggests this a pervasive problem. In stark contrast to the father quoted in Chapter Two, who described youth sports as "a meritocracy," a significant percentage of parents believe the system is rigged to give the children of well-connected individuals advantages over kids whose parents do not have as much clout.

Decisions about Playing Time

After a team's roster has been set, children have received their uniforms and the season begins, a coach then decides who will play what position and for how many minutes. This can be a delicate balancing act. It seems inevitable that some players or parents will be unhappy about their children's playing time. When parents are convinced a coach does not treat all players equally, their attitude toward sports can quickly sour.

The coaches we interviewed approached this challenge using a variety of strategies. One veteran soccer and hockey coach identified two basic objectives that can anchor decisions related to playing time: a desire to win or a commitment to equity. To illustrate this concept, he shared the following anecdote:

> I was coaching this U 9 team I really thought was U 11, but they had a board of directors and it was a B level team. Wasn't their A team, it was their B team. So it was kids who couldn't make the A team. So they put together a B team. And I said to them during a meeting, "You know, do you wanna play to win? Or do you want everybody to play? There's two types. You know, the A team's gonna probably wanna play to win." After the parents on his team decided that they wanted everybody to play, he told them, "Everybody will play thirty minutes in a game." That approach seemed to satisfy the parents.

We did observe several coaches who used similar tactics, dividing up playing time as equally as they could. This was especially common in recreational leagues for younger children. At soccer matches for seven-year-olds, for instance, an entire group of children might play for a portion of the game, then leave the field as a unit, replaced by a second squad of teammates. In some T-ball games, coaches tend to let everyone on their team play in the field at the same time, regardless of the total numbers. They are not concerned if one of their players is lounging in the outfield picking dandelions rather than watching the game, which has no declared winner or loser, because no one keeps score.

But as kids get older, the desire to win starts to take precedence over a commitment to equity. Very quickly, winning becomes the primary objective. Before players graduate from elementary school, the number of minutes they spent on the court can vary significantly. Coaches generally try to give every kid some playing time, but those minutes are not evenly distributed. Getting the right players on the field in key situations becomes more important than equal playing time.

Interestingly, very rarely did parents complain about playing time. What bothered them was the reasons certain kids got to play while others were confined to the sidelines. As one person explained to us, "In football, it starts with, you know, the coach's son is the quarterback. The kid he's passing it to or handing it off to is the other coach's son. And they both play offense and defense and they're getting all the praise. Of course, they're gonna put their son first." Another dad related that "I've seen some instances where one child who is obviously not as good as some of the other kids was getting more playing time. I think that all parents will feel that way. Proving it is a different story. These things are hard to avoid when personal relationships are involved, and those personal relationships can be deeply embedded within a community."

Addressing these situations can be especially difficult because, as the parent above points out, coaches rarely inform parents about their reasons for choosing to play some kids over others. And even if parents did have that information, they might not feel comfortable questioning a coach's decisions. Raising concerns about playing time to coaches could negatively affect a child's future opportunities with that team. Remaining silent is a safer option for most parents.

A related concern expressed by parents was the ongoing anxiety they felt about "job security." Although travel teams tend to retain a core group of players year after year, that does not mean everyone is guaranteed a lifetime membership with the club. Players are usually required to try out for their teams at the beginning of each season. Returning athletes have advantages over new applicants, but there is always a chance they could be replaced. As one mother observed, "In our area, there are three or four travel teams, so there are lots of options. But you can get kicked off a team at any time. The coach can decide to kick any player off the team." "In our town," another mother explained, "there are travel teams and community teams. About 500 kids try out every year. Out of those 500, about 350 are placed on community teams and 150 make the elite team. My son made the elite team and keeps getting better. But last year, our coach was an asshole. My son felt like he always had to impress the coach, or he could get cut."

At any point, coaches can decide that certain players are expendable. Replacing those kids with individuals perceived as more talented can give their team a competitive edge. Ambitious coaches often keep their eyes on players from other teams who might consider jumping ship. In other words, there is always a pool of players that coaches can draw from to add to—or replace—members of their clubs. Decisions about why a player is cut are rarely explained to athletes or their parents. Such uncertainty can create stress for young players who lack the power to influence the decisions made by adults.

Sources of Power

The information presented above illustrates the ways adults in positions of authority can influence the opportunities delivered to young athletes. But how do they acquire that power? What does it take to develop the clout necessary to determine which kids get to play and who is relegated to the sidelines?

One way adults increase their levels of influence is to acquire administrative positions in the leagues their children play in. As they work up the hierarchy of authority, the impact of their recommendations and decisions tends to expand. A parent might, for example, volunteer to oversee the snack stand or help coordinate a fundraising effort. Successfully carrying out that work might lead to a position on the league's board of directors. In some towns, board elections are competitive. A long list of candidates run for the board and only one or two are successful. More often, the large time commitment associated with serving on a board scares many potential candidates away. Individuals motivated to serve are welcomed onto the board with open arms. Over time, their power gradually escalates. Board members may reach out to their friends and encourage them to consider running for open seats, which can augment their power within the organization.

In theory, a board member's ability to influence team-level decisions should be minimal. A well-run organization will create structures that prevent individuals from acting unilaterally. But board policies are not always enforced consistently. The lines that divide appropriate and questionable behavior can get blurry. Because important board decisions are often made in private, families may know very little about the basis of those decisions. And when board meetings are open to the public, attendance tends to be low. Furthermore, many of the decisions that impact a young athlete's experiences are never formally discussed or voted on. Private conversations between a coach and a board member may result in one player making an all-star team while another is left off the roster. As one father told us, "I'm not stupid. I can figure it out. There's a board of directors, there's these coaches, and they're all buddy buddy. They're all working to keep certain kids in more strategic positions. I do think that at the youth level, whether it's the club or even town sports, politics and relationships play a role."

A parent's ability to question the decisions that affect her child is even more challenging when it comes to privately run teams, which tend to not be guided by publicly shared policies or procedures. Profit-driven organizations are under no obligation to respond to parent concerns or complaints. They operate as businesses, not democratic institutions that serve the public.

Nevertheless, it is possible for some parents to sway the decisions made by coaches of private clubs. This is especially true with individuals who have the resources necessary to influence team administrators; wealth and social status can amplify their voices. One father we spoke with recalled that "There was a kid who, um, his dad's a hedge fund guy and he donates a lot of money to the rink. So as a favor, the organization always puts this kid at the highest team for his age group. This kid's dad had basically been financing the rink."

The more money is involved, the greater the potential for adults to leverage their power to create advantages for their kids. And due to the costs of playing for an elite sports club, the average income of travel team parents tends to be higher than is the case with recreational leagues. This helps to explain why travel teams are concentrated in wealthy communities. As one parent noted, "When you get to wealthy areas, you have more parents that can have an undue influence on the team. That's just the way it is. Our county is like, you know, it's a wealthy area. So you have people that were dropping 100K, like investing money into a team, or something like that." The higher the average income, the more potential clients. This is why profit-driven sports organizations are often concentrated in wealthy suburbs—they follow the money.

Is This New?

The idea that not all young athletes are treated the same is not a groundbreaking revelation. For as long as organized sports have existed, coaches have given special treatment to some players and made life difficult for others. This happens at all levels of the system. Coaches often have trouble separating their relationships with players and families from their responsibilities as team leaders. This reality, though problematic, is nothing new. Parents have always used their personal relationships and connections to authority to secure advantages for their children.

It would be naïve, however, to conclude that conditions today are the same as was true a generation ago. Although adults have long complained about questionable behavior by coaches and league officials, their critiques have become more widespread and thunderous over time. Concerns about the political aspects of youth sports have gained traction in response to some fundamental shifts in the structure of the industry as well as our society's views about parenting.

When we were young, kids tended to be allowed to manage their own free time. From the hour that school let out until dinner was served, they roamed the neighborhood with little or no supervision. We both recall countless adventures that involved playing in the streets with our friends, riding bikes through the neighborhood, and brushes with danger. Most of the time, our parents had no idea what we were doing. What they didn't know didn't hurt them. This hands-off approach to parenting was common throughout much of the twentieth century.

Things started to change in the 1980s, when our culture began to redefine what it means to be a good parent. Concerns about public safety, fed by sensationalist media accounts of criminal activity, triggered widespread debates about the wisdom of allowing children to play independently. Kids with too much free time on their hands were more likely to get in trouble. To avoid this outcome, parents were encouraged to actively manage their children's social lives. Structured activities overseen by adults came to be seen as preferable to spontaneous play. *Intensive parenting,*[30] or what sociologist Sharon Hays calls *intensive mothering*[31] and sociologist Anette Lareau describes as *concerted cultivation,*[32] the idea that adults should do whatever it takes to provide opportunities for their children to succeed, became prevalent.

The shift from hands-off to intensive parenting had a powerful impact on the types of athletic activities kids participated in. In the past, parents tended to take a hands-off approach to their children's sports activities. Little was required of them after they signed up their kids to join the local swim team or AYSO soccer league. They relied on parent volunteers or school coaches to take care of their sons and daughters. During the 1980s and 1990s, that approach fell out of favor. The idea that parents should be heavily involved in managing their children's extracurricular lives became widely accepted. One way to demonstrate that they were "good parents" was to enroll their children in high status sports activities. This included things like playing for an elite team, getting private coaching, or attending summer recruiting camps held on college campuses. Proving your worth as a parent become steadily more costly and time-consuming.

At almost the same time our society was rethinking a parent's responsibilities, the youth sports industry was dramatically expanding. Ambitious entrepreneurs took advantage of this situation, creating new services to meet growing demands for specialized athletic training. An endless array of opportunities became available to families with deep pockets. Choosing not to pay for that extra clinic or training session might raise questions about your effectiveness as a parent. Parents who chose to limit the number of hours their kids spent playing sports might provoke criticism among their friends and neighbors. The chances of this occurring were actually small, but that did not prevent parents from signing up their children for all sorts of supplemental activities.

When parents dedicate so much time, energy, and money to their children's careers, they expect those investments to pay off. Why fork out hundreds of dollars for private training if your daughter isn't going to earn a starting position on the basketball team? After devoting long hours driving your son to lacrosse tournaments, shouldn't he be on the field during the clutch minutes of a match? And for many parents, we learned, the ultimate payoff on their investments is a college athletic scholarship. Anything less would be a disappointment.

When parenting is framed this way, even minor decisions can seem momentous. Deciding which team your child should play for is no longer an isolated decision but an event that will influence future opportunities. Opting not to sign up for a special clinic could leave her behind the competition. If a coach does not put her on the field at key moments in a match, she may not be seen by a college scout.

This environment can heighten parent expectations and anxiety. It influences their ideas about the purpose of youth sports and the ways they measure success. In a low-stakes Little League softball game, parents may be willing to accept decisions they don't agree with. After spending thousands of dollars on sports-related expenses, they may be less forgiving. The size of those investments may justify, in their minds, a call to a coach or board member. As is true in the world of politics, when the price of participating escalates, lobbyists find a way to influence decision makers. We tend to grudgingly accept this as an unavoidable feature of politics. In our imagination, youth sports should be immune to influence peddling. The reality is much messier.

CHAPTER EIGHT

Different Backgrounds, Different Opportunities

Mother: "Yeah, he always wanted to go
to the [high-profile regional team]."

Father: "Yes, which I hear is like $6,000 or $7,000 and
that's without going to all over the place. That's before
the travel; that's just the try outs. It's before try outs,
before the travel starts."

Mother: "We're pretty much the only ones who didn't try out
for them. Why have him try out and you're going to say no."

— *Parents of a travel baseball player* —

Sports has long been considered a fundamental component of American culture, taking on almost mythic significance. Scoring the winning touchdown for your high school or hitting a walk off home run in an important Little League game seem to symbolize the best parts of our society. For as long as we can remember, scenes like these have captivated moviegoers of all ages—the dramatic comeback of the underdog basketball team in *Hoosiers*, the unexpected success of the ragtag players on the *Bad News Bears*, or the gold medal performance of the US hockey team in *Miracle on Ice.* Sports provide opportunities for young athletes to triumph over adversity. All that is required is hard work and dedication.

Movies like those mentioned above reinforce the image of sports as a level playing field, open to all competitors regardless of their personal characteristics or backgrounds. Athletic success, after all, is decided on the playing field. The person or team with the most talent or the most grit is destined to win first prize. That view of human potential anchors the American Dream. It inspires hope among citizens of all ages and nurtures our belief that anything is possible.

This idealistic perspective on athletics may be comforting, but it fails to capture the realities of the youth sports industry today. Although opportunities to compete can potentially open doors for young athletes, not all kids have equal access. Through our research, we discovered that talent alone does not determine an athlete's likelihood of success. Their gender, ethnicity, and economic background can all impact their careers in sports. That has been true, to some extent, for as long as kids have participated in organized athletics. Most of the characters depicted in the movies referred to above, for example, are white boys or men. But disparities in access to sports has increased substantially over the past forty years. Children from families that lack the appropriate resources must hurdle barriers that seem to get higher by the year.

In many places, athletes short on money or social capital lose out to their more privileged peers. Commercialization of the youth sports industry has heightened those divisions. In many locations, simply paying the sign-up fees and attending practices is no longer enough to provide young athletes with opportunities to show what they can do. While conducting research for this book, we were surprised at the lengths some parents go to provide their children with advantages—signing up their kids for individual coaching sessions, sending them to showcase tournaments in other states, and hiring consultants to create recruiting files. Families who cannot afford to pay for these supplemental services can be at a real disadvantage.

In this chapter, we look closely at how race, class, gender, and neighborhood all affect the decisions made by parents of young athletes. We focus on how youth sports create opportunities and advantages for certain families and make it difficult for others to remain in the game. Few of the parents we interviewed were aware of that situation when they signed up their children to play organized sports for the first time. Like most of us, they assumed their children would have the same chances to score the winning goal or receive awards for exemplary performance as their peers.

Changes Over Time

Although parents of current athletes are likely to have strong memories of their own experiences playing sports, those recollections are connected to structures and practices that no longer anchor the world of youth sports. This is due to significant changes that have occurred over the last half-century. As a result of those changes, opportunities provided to young athletes, expectations for players, and definitions of athletic success all look quite different than was the case a generation ago.

Until the middle of the twentieth century, most sporting experiences for children were provided by organizations like the YMCA/YWCA, Boys and Girls Scouts, and Boys and Girls Clubs. Children participated in local, neighborhood-based programs that charged minimal fees. Practices and games were held in public parks or on school fields, overseen by volunteer coaches. The number of kids who participated in those programs expanded rapidly during the 1950s and 1960s, as members of the Baby Boomer generation became interested in sports. By the early 1960s, Little League Baseball branches had been established in all fifty states and many countries around the world. Most organized sports, however, were offered to white boys only.

Things began to change after Title IX was adopted in 1972 and gender-based discrimination in any education program that receives funding from the federal government was prohibited. The desegregation of Little League Baseball just two years later added momentum to the push for more inclusive approaches to youth sports. Children who might previously have been excluded from joining local teams due to the color of their skin were encouraged to participate alongside their peers. Breaking down barriers that previously prevented large numbers of kids from playing sports helped to drive growth of the industry in the years that followed.

At the same time the youth sports industry was expanding, its structure was shifting. Tax cuts enacted in the 1980s hit the industry hard. The budgets of publicly funded programs for kids were slashed, forcing schools and recreation departments around the country to overhaul their budgets. Athletic activities were trimmed or eliminated. This created an immense gap that needed to be filled. Parents who wanted to keep their children active were forced to look for new options.

Savvy private entrepreneurs capitalized on this situation. Recognizing that demand for youth sports programs was not being met, they stepped in to fill the void. Driven by all sorts of reasons, they formed private teams, leagues, and specialized training options for young athletes. To maximize profits, they offered programs that ran throughout the year. Those options were appealing for a couple of reasons. First, they created a dependable routine for families. If parents knew their kids would be at basketball practices every Monday, Wednesday, and Saturday, they wouldn't have to search for other activities to fill their schedules. Another aspect of privately organized sports that made them desirable was their exclusivity. Anyone can sign up to play AYSO soccer, but private teams screened potential players. Only the individuals who met their standards were selected for membership. Athletes chosen to join elite teams could then receive higher level coaching and compete against talented athletes from other cities and states. In this environment, the "travel team" became ingrained in American culture.

Unequal Access

From that point on, youth sports became steadily more expensive, intense, and hierarchical. The menu of options available to athletes seemed limitless. New teams, leagues, tournaments, and coaching clinics formed across the country. Young athletes interested in acquiring a competitive edge could play for teams that competed year-round. Private trainers were more than willing to help them hone their skills. Those developments spurred increases in the number of kids who participated in organized sports throughout the 1980s and 1990s.

However, statistics that capture increases in overall participation rates fail to capture the whole story. Not all young children benefited from growth of the youth sports industry. As the system became more profit-driven, the costs of advancing through the athletic pipeline climbed. In contrast with community-based leagues, which are staffed by volunteers, commercial organizations are usually run by adults whose income depends on their success. Attracting new customers will increase their chances of survival. Similar to your local cable television provider, a commercial sports enterprise will generate larger profits if they convince subscribers to pay for the gold package rather than the basic option.

We recognize that many professional coaches and trainers care deeply about their clients. Even the most dedicated individuals, however, are subject to the realities of the system. A coach who advises potential customers to play for a local recreational team rather the company that pays his paycheck could soon be out of a job. As one person told us, professional coaches are "being paid to produce winning programs. Because why would you spend $4,500 to send your kid to a pay-to-play program if they're not going to be the winning team that's going to be recognized when the college coaches come to look at them?"

These changes in the structure of the youth sports industry had a powerful influence on the ways young athletes structured their time, the expectations placed on them, and the decisions parents made. As we have described, commercialization of youth sports increased the pressure placed on kids to set themselves apart from their peers. Before they graduate from elementary school, many children feel obligated to sign up for activities designed to accelerate their athletic development—and attract the attention of coaches and scouts. That could involve playing for an elite travel club or signing up to train with a private coach. In many locations, playing in a local recreational league or earning a spot on a school team is no longer considered enough. Specializing in a single sport at an early age has become the norm rather than the exception.

Many parents would like to follow that pathway but lack the resources required to do so. As youth sports shifted from a community-based to a profit-driven model, a family's socioeconomic background increasingly determined the decisions they made for their children.

Middle class parents tend to invest significant amounts of time, money, and energy in their children's extracurricular activities than do families with limited disposable incomes. This helps to explain the steady decline in athletic participation among certain segments of the population over the past thirty years. One study found that 33.9 percent of children from the lowest income households play organized sports, compared with 67.7 percent of kids from the wealthiest families.[33]

As we might expect, race and class are often linked when it comes to athletics. Children who are poor, or from Black or Hispanic households, are less likely to participate in organized sports than white kids. A number of factors are responsible for the disparities. The most obvious is affordability. After paying the rent and buying groceries, many parents simply do not have the funds to finance their children's athletic careers. For such families, growth in private club-based sports has reduced the options available to their children. Time constraints, limited access to athletic facilities, and parental priorities can also make it difficult for low-income and minority children to participate in sports.[34]

A Ground Level View

Although unequal access to sports has been a reality for decades, the "pay-to-play" model that became prevalent during the 1980s and 1990s exacerbated the situation. As community-based programs were eliminated and neighborhood fields paved over, low-income kids fell further and further behind their wealthier classmates. What does that look like in practice? How are actual players and families affected by the growing influence of money in kids' sports?

As we conducted the research for this book, we observed evidence of growing inequality in sports on many levels. One striking sign of change was the diminishing status of low-cost, community-based sports. In the area that we live, recreational sports are struggling for survival. When our own kids were in elementary school, Little League Baseball/Softball was thriving. Towns in the area fielded multiple teams in each age bracket. Less than a decade later, several of those cities can no longer field enough teams to form a league. Some do not have enough players to form a single team. To cope with this reality, several towns joined forces to create a region- rather than town-based league. Furthermore, many kids are deciding not to play in that league. At younger and younger ages, young athletes are opting to play for travel teams that compete against clubs from other cities, counties, and states.

Not everyone is signing up to play for private clubs though. In our area, travel team players as well as the fans who supported them tended to be white and economically stable. The amount of time and money they invested in kids' sports was substantial. Families were required to shuttle their children to practices two or three times a week, and weekends were often dominated by tournament play. Adults who worked in the evenings or on weekends, had to find other parents who could chauffeur their children to team events. They were also expected to serve shifts at concession stands, attend parent meetings, and help with fundraising. As one parent told us, "When you join a travel team, the whole family joins the team, so you really need to think about time and the expense. It's more than they tell you it's going to be, because it's hotels, food, movies when you're at the hotel, the traveling time. So it's a lot of stuff. I think when we joined, they said it would be about a thousand dollars for the season, but it's much more than that." Another parent remarked, "Make sure your kid likes the game and enjoys coming out here because it's an extra commitment. Not only in time, because you've got that extra practice, but you're also traveling more. So they've got to be willing to commit to that. And it's more money. We go to tournaments. That's more money. And when we go to these tournaments, if it's overnight, that's hotel costs. So you need more money and more commitment."

How much money did parents spend on their children's athletic activities? The costs ranged from a couple of hundred dollars to upwards of $30,000 per season, depending on age of the athlete, sport played, and level of competition. What we found particularly interesting was a general mismatch between estimated and actual costs of playing on a travel team. For example, one question on a survey we distributed to more than 400 parents at soccer and basketball tournaments asked them how much money they spent on one child's sports activities in a year. The average amount supplied was $1,200. But when we asked individuals to list all of their sports-related expenses, the numbers they came up with far surpassed their initial estimates. Here is one example of a modified budget created by one of the parents we interviewed:

Participation fees	$5,000
Equipment	$500
Hotel rooms at tournaments	$2,000
Food at tournaments	$1,000
Transportation costs	$500
Total cost	**$9,000 per season**

After performing these calculations, the parent remarked that "a lot of parents just look at it and it's for their kid, so they don't care. They don't really keep track of it." Other conversations we had with parents confirmed that observation.

For some parents, allocating large sums of money to their children's extracurricular activities may not be an issue. Many of the people we spoke to believed the benefits their kids derived from elite training justified the costs. They were happy to invest in their children's athletic development. But it's important to recognize that not all families can afford to sign up their children to play for privately run teams. No matter how much parents would like to support their children's athletic careers, the costs associated with travel sports may prevent them from even considering that option.

Defraying the Costs

In a democratic society committed to equal opportunity, it would seem reasonable to assume that financial aid would be available to families that cannot afford to cover the costs of travel sports. If teams are committed to fielding the most competitive team possible, wouldn't they offer scholarships to talented athletes from low-income families? If so, how much support might a financially strapped player receive?

We would like to offer clear and unequivocal answers to these questions, but, unfortunately, we cannot. That is not a result of a lack of effort on our part. In interview after interview, we asked parents and team managers about the financial support available to financially challenged players. We also searched for that information on team websites. Our efforts were futile. Some people made statements like "I'm sure that scholarships are available," or "When we know a player is struggling financially, we pitch in to help cover their costs." But no one could provide concrete details about scholarships or the process of applying for financial support.

Although we did manage to locate statistics about the percentage of athletes who receive athletic scholarships to play in the NCAA and the number of students in America who play high school basketball, we could not locate basic information about scholarship support available to kids who play on travel teams. This situation highlights another dimension of inaccessibility in profit–driven sports. Recreational leagues usually provide families with reliable information about the costs of participating in a sport. Typically, parents will shell out some money for a baseball glove or snacks, but those costs are minimal. When it comes to teams run by private organizations, those costs are difficult to pinpoint, as are the steps a parent should take to apply for financial support.

We believe many privately run organizations do offer scholarships to financially strapped families. Few, however, are willing to make that information public. Parents should not have to work so diligently to determine the costs of playing for a particular team. Information about financial aid should be easily accessible. Families who struggle financially or do not speak English fluently might find that process intimidating. When forced to ask for help, they could decide to give up on their plans to pursue opportunities that more privileged families can secure for their children with minimal effort.

Opportunities for Female Athletes

For years, the opportunities available to athletically inclined girls were limited. Most organized sports catered to the needs of boys. Treated as second class citizens, girls were expected to invest their energies in activities that did not place physical demands on them. Things began to change in 1972, when Title IX was adopted. Since that time, participation rates among female athletes have climbed. Between 1973 and 1994, the number of girls who played sports almost doubled. In 2020, 52 percent of all girls in the US played at least one sport, only 2 percentage points lower than is true for boys.[35]

How has commercialization of the youth sports industry affected the athletic pursuits of girls and young women? Has the momentum generated by enactment of Title IX continued to grow?

What barriers have they overcome and what challenges do they continue to face?

The research we conducted for this book highlights the positive impact of Title IX but also reveals some troubling realities. Although Title IX opened doors for many female athletes, not all girls could take advantage of those opportunities. White girls are four times as likely than athletes of any other race to participate in organized sports.[36] And it might not surprise you to learn that many female athletes of color are left behind because they can't afford to participate. The costs of playing travel ball price them out of the market. Most travel clubs are based in predominantly white communities where the cost of living is high. When girls of color do play, they are likely to compete in basketball or track and field. Sports like tennis, swimming, and lacrosse attract primarily white middle-class participants.

In the area of New York where we live, girls are almost as likely as boys to play sports. The female athletes we observed and interviewed were taking advantage of increased access to athletics as well as widespread support for the idea that girls have what it takes to excel on the athletic field. They invested an enormous amount of time and energy in sports. This often forced them to make sacrifices—missing birthday parties, summer camp, sleepovers with friends. Nevertheless, they skillfully juggled social, academic, and athletic commitments.

The parents we interviewed recognized the demands their daughters faced but also emphasized the benefits of taking sports seriously. One idea they mentioned frequently related to the effects of spending so much time in spaces that did not include boys. At athletic events, they did not have to compete with boys for time or attention. Team captains were all girls. Winning baskets were scored by girls. In difficult situations, they turned to other girls for support. The sense of camaraderie that developed could be quite empowering. When confronted with challenges, they worked with other girls to accomplish their goals. As one parent explained, "They're working as a team and it's instilled in them that they have a responsibility to the team, a work ethic, and they had to work together to take it to the next level."

Although athletes develop relationships with their teammates in all sorts of settings, the intensity of playing travel sports can accelerate that process. Seasons extend for months and players often remain with the same team for several years. Friendships may deepen over weekends spent in tournament hotels. In some cases, friction developed between teammates, but those conflicts rarely festered.

Parents told us the bonds their daughters formed with their teammates through practice, competition, and travel served as a valued source of strength for them. Players pushed each other to reach their potential, and that dynamic provided them with the support that helped them do so. As one mother related, "My daughter really feels, 'This is who I am. I'm a soccer player.' It's great for building her self-esteem and building her confidence. It's just a great thing for her." Concerned about widespread depression among adolescents in our society, parents related that playing sports provided their daughters with a dependable source of stability. "You read about eating disorders that go on," one mother related, "and cutting and horrible stuff, and I think our daughters' playing sports is keeping them in a safe place in terms of habits. My daughter has a healthy opinion of her body. It's a strong and athletic machine."

The adults we interviewed highlighted all sorts of ways that playing for a travel team helped their daughters grow. But it is important to recognize that those parents had the resources necessary to support their daughters' athletic ambitions. They dedicated considerable amounts of time and money to sports. Most of the parents could be described as middle class, and most of them were white—more so than was the case for recreational leagues in the area. In an ideal world, girls would have the chance to play for highly regarded sports teams, regardless of their race or economic background. The reality is much more complicated. The shift from community-based to profit-driven sports has reduced the opportunities for large numbers of girls whose parents cannot afford to pay thousands of dollars each year to support their daughters' athletic careers. And girls whose families can cover the costs of travel sports often discover that playing on an elite team may be more stressful than they had anticipated. These factors help to explain why girls drop out of sports at twice the rate of boys.[37]

Persistent Inequity

Parents of young athletes hope their children will have the chance to prove themselves on the playing field—and their success will be determined by their talent and effort. For decades, that was not the case. Deep-seated racism and sheer ignorance created a system that supported the dreams of white male athletes. Discrimination against girls and athletes of color was overt and pervasive. Leagues denied children who did not embody the characteristics they valued from joining their ranks. In the world of youth sports, girls and athletes of color were treated as second class citizens.

During the Civil Right Movement, the tide appeared to be turning. The push for equality in all aspects of social life led to significant changes in the sporting world. Events like the adoption of Title IX and desegregation of Little League Baseball created enticing opportunities for young athletes who had previously been excluded from most organized sports. Their eagerness to take advantage of those opportunities drove steady expansion of the youth sports industry in the years that followed. The playing field appeared to have been leveled.

Just a few years later, the system underwent another transformation. The shift from community-based sports to privately run clubs had profound effects on the activities that young athletes participated in. Families could no longer depend on local nonprofit organizations to support their children. Private clubs steadily become more prevalent and desirable. In the wake of those changes, profit rather than altruism became the guiding force. Entrepreneurs established private clubs in areas where they could charge steep fees, which they did. Opportunities in wealthy neighborhoods increased but diminished in areas that struggled economically.

Today, overt racial discrimination has been replaced by economic segregation that is often difficult to spot. Rates of sports participation are tightly linked with family income. Elite teams allow children of any race, gender, or economic background to try out. Yet many families lack the resources or knowledge to take advantage of those opportunities. Joining a travel team is simply too expensive or places too many demands on families for that to be a realistic option for them.

The youth sports system that exists today offers the façade of democratic opportunity that is undercut by economic inequity. That surface level openness makes it difficult to change. No laws or regulations prevent certain families from participating, but the daily challenges they face makes it all but impossible for their kids to play for certain teams. If a young athlete manages to earn a spot on an elite club, she might not be able to afford the supplementary training or private coaching that help her teammates develop. The system seems to constantly metastasize, spawning new profit-generating branches that make it difficult for economically challenged kids to thrive. A young softball player or swimmer might be loaded with talent. Her drive to excel might set her apart from her peers. But her fate might ultimately be determined by the neighborhood she lives in or the size of her parent's paycheck.

CHAPTER NINE

Navigating Change
How Parents Adjust When Their Children Stop Playing Sports

"I think I took it harder than he did. I enjoyed the travel baseball. I liked the group of people. I liked the circle of parents. I was kinda like missing it more than he was probably when he stopped going."

— Travel baseball parent —

"I'm hoping that most parents that are involved at this level understand that it will end. It will end in the next couple of years. So how does it continue. And the only way it really continues is what they bring from that to the next journey in life."

— High school sports parent —

The arc of an athlete's athletic career tends to follow a natural progression. In the early stages, the demands placed on them are minimal, and the emphasis is on having fun. As the player matures, those demands gradually escalate. Children as well as their parents can gradually adjust to the new expectations placed on them. The adults we spoke with often contrasted their children's experiences playing travel sports with the more carefree approach to town-based athletics, but the increase in intensity they described unfolded over a period of years.

For many parents, it feels like they have been riding a bicycle up a steep mountain, steadily exerting more effort to reach the pinnacle. That goal keeps them focused and committed. Although they experience struggles, the accolades and awards they receive along the way justify those hardships.

At the end, everything changes.

Upon reaching the top of the mountain, parents of athletes do not usually enjoy the luxury of coasting down to the point where they began their ride. Instead, their bicycles are taken away and they must figure out how to get back down on their own. They may have known, at some level, that they would eventually reach that point, but the actual experience is often quite jarring. After pursuing a clearly defined goal for so many years, they are challenged to reorient their activities, while their children move on to the next stages of their lives on their own. Although all parents must grapple with the challenges associated with this type of separation, the experience is acutely felt by adults who have attached so much importance to a single activity—youth sports.

In this chapter, we look at the experiences of parents as they respond to the end of their children's athletic careers. As they reflect on the experiences with travel sports, what events seem particularly significant to them? In what ways did their ideas about athletics evolve? We discovered that in looking back at events associated with travel sports, parents made insightful observations about their children's development as athletes and as people. Those comments also highlight the realities of parenting in a society that has become increasingly hierarchical, competitive, and achievement oriented. As we will show, travel sports provide an anchor for many adults as they attempt to create a sense of stability and purpose in their lives as parents. However, when their children move on to other pursuits, it also can create a void that proves difficult to fill.

Milestones: Celebrations, Ceremonies, and Grieving

"I guess I'd have to say the ones that stand out in my mind are the ones where they won a championship of some sort, just because it feels magical. This is a lot like the past season with the soccer team—it feels magical. Your feelings are all positive and good and they stay with you, you remember them. Regardless of how much the coach may have had to do with that level of success. You think of them fondly in the future."

Up to this point, we have focused almost exclusively on the actions and emotions that sports evoke in parents while they are immersed in their children's athletic lives. From that position, immediate events tend to have a strong influence on the ways adults process those activities. For example, after a particularly exhilarating or disappointing game, a parent might focus on the significance of that contest. As we conducted the research for this book, we made an effort to speak with parents in as many different settings as possible, to capture the full range of their thoughts about youth sports. One approach that proved especially helpful was to talk with parents at the beginnings and ends of sport seasons. At those points in time, they could step back and reflect on competitive sports with a broader frame of reference.

Most of the adults we interviewed had children in high school. By that point, their sons and daughters had been playing sports for several years. Over that period of time, the parents had extensive experience overseeing their children's athletic lives. And over time, their views about competitive sports, and its effects on their families, had evolved. Goals, priorities, and opinions all shifted.

One thing that became clear to us was that by the time their children had entered high school, most parents had started to think about where travel sports was leading their kids—and themselves. At that point, the conclusions of athletic careers were coming into sharper focus. This led them to think carefully about the long-term consequences of the decisions they had made over the years. Engaging in that process encouraged them to consider not only the next steps their children would take—but how their own lives would change after the last travel team game had concluded as well.

American culture encourages that kind of contemplation, especially when it comes to sports. As young athletes near the end of key stages in the careers, they are expected to take part in a series of events designed to celebrate their accomplishments and to bring a sense of closure to their attachment to teams. Rituals such as senior day, final home game ceremonies, and team banquets all serve this purpose. Similar to graduation ceremonies that take place in high school auditoriums, they provoke a range of emotions: exuberance, nostalgia, sadness, and accomplishment. As the youth sports industry has expanded, these rituals have become integral components of an athlete's career, as dependable as opening day ceremonies and homecoming games. They underscore the significance of key transition points in the lives of young athletes.

At these events, the spotlight remains focused on the retiring athletes, yet parents are almost always involved in some way. At senior days, for example, parents often walk to the center of the playing field with their children, are presented with bouquets, and have their pictures taken together. End-of-season awards ceremonies almost always include comments delivered by players and coaches about the invaluable role parents played in the accomplishments of their daughters and sons.

We discovered that parents responded to the impending final stages of their children's athletic careers in a variety of ways. Some expressed relief that they would no longer be required to chauffeur their kids to practices and tournaments. Others focused on key accomplishments or games that remained etched in their memories. Some experienced what could be described as a period of grieving; formal celebrations of the ends of careers heightened a sense of loss that had been building in previous months. After organizing their lives around sports for years, it was difficult to imagine what their lives would be like without the dependable rhythm of practices, games, and tournaments.

For parents in their forties and fifties, the task of reconstructing social lives independent of their children seemed daunting. Even though they knew the end would eventually come, that awareness did not lessen the impact. As one father of a recently retired baseball player shared with us, "We did sit around and ask ourselves what we're going to do on Sundays, and what are we going to do this summer? Because of that, we will miss it. We will definitely miss going to the games. That, I think, will be the biggest thing, and not seeing him play. But I'm sure we can get involved in something. Life goes on. You change."

To cope with the disruptions they were facing, parents relied on a wide variety of coping strategies. Some individuals, for example, created scrapbooks that memorialized their children's athletic careers. Reviewing photographs and mementos collected over a period of years allowed them to relive key moments and to create a lasting record of their experiences. Some parents of retired athletes returned to the fields where their children once played, to imbibe the atmosphere associated with courts no longer buzzing with activity. Others continued to attend games, clad in team jerseys or hats, even though their children no longer played for those teams. As one parent told us, "We can still stop by the field and watch a game. We've gone to Little League games and watched kids play." This father, like many of the parents we interviewed, was not ready to let go of memories associated with his son's childhood, even after their children graduated from high school. At that point, they came to appreciate formative events from the past that they might not have fully appreciated in real time. Looking back, they could decide which memories to preserve and which to discard. The process of reflection kept them connected to people and places that had played such a central role in their lives—to move on without completely letting go.

Looking Forward, Looking Back
In our interviews, parents seemed to appreciate the opportunity to reflect on their experiences with sports and to evaluate the positive

and negative aspects of those experiences. As they assessed the impact of sports on their families, parents seemed to appreciate the opportunity to think carefully about activities that anchored their lives but that they rarely questioned or analyzed. Although individual parents focused on different aspects of the travel sports experience, there were some common themes that emerged from their comments, which we will discuss here.

One topic that came up repeatedly in our discussions with parents was the value of the travel sports experience. As we have noted, interviewees frequently emphasized the high costs, in money and in time, associated with youth sports. Few parents fully understood the depth of the commitment they were making when they signed up their children to play on a travel team. Initially, that realization could be quite jarring. Over time, though, parents tended to focus less on the costs and more on the long-term impact sports would have on their children. This was especially true of adults whose children were nearing the ends of their athletic careers. As they approached those milestones, their priorities seemed to shift.

Almost all of the adults we interviewed told us they felt that signing up their children for a travel team had been a wise decision. Even those who complained about the high costs associated with the experience (which many parents did), indicated that their children were better athletes and people as a result of the challenges they faced through travel sports. Of course our pool of interviewees did not include many parents whose children had left their travel teams; those people might have expressed more critical opinions about youth sports. But it is also worth noting that the number of families that decided to leave the teams we followed was fairly small—one or two each season.

When asked to talk about the positive and negative aspects of competitive sports, parents often began by comparing community-based leagues with travel teams. In those comparisons, they usually noted that travel sports demanded more of young athletes, and their children benefited from that escalation in expectations.

For example, when asked why her daughter had joined a travel team, one parent responded that "The competition was at a higher standard and she was ready for the next level of play. The town team was wonderful, but then they get to the point where they need some more competition, a higher level of play." This parent, like many we interviewed, focused on the ways that travel sports helped their sons and daughters develop as athletes. According to another person we spoke with, "The travel team brought a skill level that he just wasn't going to get elsewhere. So I think that was the real benefit, that it challenged him more. We knew that it was a travel team that was going to play other towns where you had to try out, so that the skill level was higher."

After mentioning the athletic benefits of playing on a travel team, though, most parents moved on to talk about ways their children had grown as human beings as a result of playing on more competitive teams. Over time, those less tangible benefits took on greater significance for the adults we interviewed. Physical development was almost assumed. It was the reason they decided to move their children from town-based to travel teams. During our interviews, however, parents of adolescents talked about the life lessons their children acquired through sports in greater depth than they did about athletic accomplishments. It appeared that as they watched their children's athletic careers unfold, their focus shifted from specific accomplishments—getting a clutch hit or winning an important game—to the habits of mind that would be useful to them off the field. In this way, their orientation moved from the present to the future. Parents who often appeared emotionally invested in the outcomes of particular games became quite contemplative when given the space to step back and think about what they truly wanted their children to accomplish. The following comments illustrate this pattern:

- "It's more about the process than the actual result. It's about commitment, working hard, as opposed to just going out there and scoring a goal or winning. I don't worry as much about winning. I mean it is important, but I put a bigger emphasis on all of the things you do to prepare yourself for that game."

• "I'm not hoping for a college scholarship. So I guess what I would hope for would be those life lessons. Those life lessons that we talked about—about being dedicated, about raising the bar for herself, and the lifelong friendships she's gonna have coming out of this are just going to be amazing, I think."

• "This is great, this is great character-building stuff, you know. So I know my son's not going to be a professional baseball player, there's no chance of that. However, he's been on the mound many times, many times he had to live through those situations and survived them, and there are situations where he screwed up and there are situations where he didn't. And experience gained from both of those things is not replaceable, you're not going to get it from sitting in a classroom, you know."

• "If you want something and you want to be good at something you know, you have to work hard at it. I think, you know, in the end it's a great experience, life experience, just for them learning just how to deal with people, how to work hard, and how to deal with life issues so I think it's a really great thing."

• "It's all about the life skills that go with this, and you gotta have fun, and you gotta make it enjoyable for you and your child. But also use it as a way to learn life skills. I have two daughters, and I grew up with all boys, and I'm hard on my girls, not because I'm trying to be mean but because I want them to be self-sufficient, and I want them to be motivated. I want them to have the self-confidence to carry themselves in all different sorts of situations."

As their children advanced through the system, parents started to view sports activities as components of an athletic career, rather than as isolated incidents. Practices, conversations with coaches, interactions with other players, and athletic competitions were all seen as steps leading their children toward something larger. As the endpoints of careers neared, parents paid increasing attention to the ways that athletics were preparing their children to respond to challenges they would face in the future. That broader perspective seemed to reduce the disappointment they may have felt upon discovering their early dreams of becoming the next Megan Rapinoe or Derek Jeter wasn't going to be met.

Another idea adults came to appreciate over time was the significance of the relationships that had been formed through travel sports. Spending so much time together, sometimes over more than a decade, adults as well as children formed bonds with their peers that proved enduring. A few parents told us about individual players who had criticized or bullied their children, but those comments were far outnumbered by expressions of appreciation. One parent told us that what she most appreciated about travel sports was "the soccer family—the family of girls and the family of coaches. My daughter feels very accepted and loved and cared about. And I think it's because of the focus on team, not the single person, but that everybody contributes, everybody is treated equally."

To varying degrees, parents attached to all the teams we followed observed the relationships that had formed among players provided a sense of stability to their children. The intensity of travel sports seemed to force adolescents to rely on each other to an extent not common in other situations. Through activities both on the field and off, they had developed a sense of camaraderie that helped them respond to difficult situations, to avoid engaging in risky behavior, and to push themselves to become better people. Several parents told us their children relied on their teammates more often than they did classmates from school. As one father related, "Everyone on the team may not be best friends, but they all have each other's backs, and I think that's huge. The lifelong friendships she's gonna have coming out of this are going to be amazing, I think."

Strengthening Family Bonds

Parents also valued the ways that travel sports strengthened their relationships with their sons and daughters. The sheer volume of time set aside for team activities provided sustained opportunities for them to talk with their children about a variety of topics. Long hours spent driving to games, weekends cooped up in hotels, and gaps between tournament games all created spaces for conversation. The degree to which adults took advantages of those opportunities varied, of course. In some cases, electronic devices tended to fill in those openings. But many parents referred to discussions they had with their children that might not have occurred if they had not been confined to bounded spaces for such extended periods of time.

Those conversations covered a wide range of topics. Often, they began with a review of key moments from a recently played game. One father, for example, related that "We'll come home and always talk about the games. He'll talk about something specific, 'Remember when this happened, remember when that happened.' You know, talk about the team in general. It's different things, recaps of games, how he thinks they're going to do."

Conversations that initially focused on games frequently developed into broader exchanges about other topics. In this way, athletic events provided a segue into deeper issues that might not otherwise have been broached. Parents often aspire to engage in conversations about complex issues with their children but feel unsure about how to do so. When faced with uncertainty, they may hesitate to initiate conversations about complex topics or let conversations die. Confined to a car for hours on end, they lack easy escape routes; neither the parent nor the child can simply leave the room when they feel unsure about the direction a discussion is taking.

Parents told us this led to many unplanned yet valuable conversations with their kids. Time and space allowed them to address important topics that did not come up naturally in their daily lives. In many cases, those discussions were connected to the life lessons we discuss above. After reviewing a key moment in a game, adults encouraged their children to think about how they might have approached that situation differently or what they learned from the event. Analysis of a play that did not go as planned was followed by conversations about the importance of persistence, teamwork, and overcoming failure. Parents recognized those exchanges were especially valuable at a time when online activities have made it more challenging for them to establish open communication channels with their children.

Parents appreciated those opportunities for extended conversation especially as their children got older. They told us the amount of time they spent discussing life lessons with their children increased over time. This pattern seemed to parallel the shift from the present to the future that we describe above. Winning continued to be the most immediate goal, but for many, acquiring skills that would prove valuable to their children after they stopped playing organized sports was also high on the list. This shift in perspective influenced the way adults thought about sports and added depth to their interactions with their children. In a sense, they were adjusting their goals and priorities to fit the challenges all members would be facing in the near future. Winning the next game became less of a priority. Instead, adults sought, consciously and intuitively, to prepare their sons and daughters to meet challenges they would face in college, in the workplace, and in their communities. Although few of the parents we interviewed stated so explicitly, this shift in focus also helped them to prepare for the lives they would lead after their children left their homes.

Closure

The conclusions of athletic seasons—and careers—have always served as milestones in the lives of children. Those events, however, have taken on increased significance as a result of the intensification of youth sports that has taken place over the last twenty years. For many adolescents, playing a particular sport is no longer one of many extracurricular activities that fill their schedules; it occupies more of their time than any other endeavor outside of school. In previous generations, adolescents commonly engaged in a range of activities throughout the year. At the end of one season, they shifted their focus to other pursuits. Expansion of travel sports has disrupted that sense of balance, at earlier and earlier stages in an athlete's career.

As a result of that concentration of effort and attention, the adjustments children make when athletic careers come to an end is more acutely felt than was common only a few years ago. And while the athletes are most directly affected by these shifts, parents must also grapple with the uncertainty that accompanies change. One notable difference in their experiences is that for adolescents, the end of a sports career is one of many adjustments they will make in their lives. Although the idea that when one door closes another opens is somewhat of a cliché, it seems to fit in this situation. After high school students compete in their final match, they can look forward to entering college, starting a new job, making new friends, pursuing different activities.

For parents, in contrast, severing ties to the travel team has a greater sense of finality, especially if they do not have younger children. As one parent observed, "I think it creates this sort of false bubble. At a certain point you're going to have to come out of it. It's not going to last forever." After spending ten, eleven, or twelve years supporting their children's athletic development, parents may not have a clear sense of how they will fill that time. It is much easier to reinvent yourself at the age of eighteen than it is at fifty. As they described the demands associated with travel sports, parents indicated that athletic events had created an organizational structure for their lives. Decisions about when to schedule doctor appointments, birthday parties, family vacations, and shopping trips were all made with reference to athletic schedules. When kids stop playing sports competitively, that system of activities, which had been fine-tuned over years, was disrupted; parents were forced to rethink the configuration of their daily lives.

When their children neared the ends of their careers on their travel teams, parents began to think more about life without sports. The adults we spoke with reflected on that transition with a mixture of nostalgia, appreciation, and sadness. In a conversation one of us had with three mothers of soccer players, we asked them how they would respond when their sons stopped playing the sport. "I think I'll cry. Really. That will be hard," one responded. "I will be saddened if he decides not to play in college, to be honest, but I'll understand," commented another. "I can't even fathom that," added the third.

We do not mean to imply that parents obsessively focused all of their energies on the athletic careers of their children. Some mothers and fathers attended games and tournaments, but also set aside time to participate in activities disconnected from youth sports. One mother, for example, participated in long distance running competitions for adults. Other adults we interviewed volunteered regularly for local nonprofit organizations. Those individuals seemed less intimidated by the prospect of adapting to their post-travel-sports lives. Because they had not devoted as much attention to youth sports, the void they would have to eventually fill was not as large.

Yet all parents, at some point, had to face the reality that their children would eventually move on to lives that did not center on sports or their family members. In reflecting on their children's athletic careers, they tended to focus on the positive memories they had formed rather than the difficulties they had encountered. What initially seemed like excessive commitments gradually came to provide a valued sense of rhythm and stability to their lives. In a society that increasingly seemed perplexing, parents had come to depend on the regularity of activities and relationships that sports provided. One father related that "People say to me from time to time, 'You spent an entire weekend watching baseball tournaments?' Yeah, and it was awesome! We loved it. My mom brings her chair out. It's like, it's just what we love." "I don't like to miss tournaments," explained another parent. "I like to cheer them on the sidelines. They really are fun—when they go out on the field they're fun to watch. They give 110 percent. It's a whole social aspect too. It's very social. I like the parents. So it's fun. We all have a good time. I miss it if I don't go."

One common thread that tied all the parents together, regardless of their connections to their children's travel teams, was a belief that travel sports had brought them closer to their children, which they seemed to genuinely appreciate. Many had not initially planned on devoting so much time or attention to their children's athletic lives. In retrospect, though, those investments had paid off, even though they may not have appreciated the benefits of what were often intense commitments to competitive athletics. Time tended to smooth over the rough edges of those experiences. As one mother responded when asked what advice she would give to a parent thinking of signing up their child for travel sports: "Sit back and enjoy it. The thought of it is scarier than actually doing it. When you start out, you may not realize what you're getting into, but it all works out. Just enjoy it, because it goes by really fast."

CHAPTER TEN

Advice from Experienced Adults/Words of Wisdom

"No one's been a parent before, so you don't know what you're doing until you experience it yourself. We all make mistakes and need to learn from those mistakes. It's just part of being a parent."

— *Travel soccer parent* —

Most of the people we interviewed had been involved in the world of youth sports for years or even decades. Almost all of them told us that their views about athletics had shifted as they learned more about the system. One common theme that ran through all of our discussions related to the commercialization of youth sports and the impact that development had on them and their families. Another factor that influenced people's thinking about sports was the insights they gained through experience. Over time, their perspectives broadened. Through the numerous games they observed, the different people they interacted with, and their exposure to multiple layers of the youth sports industry, they developed a foundation of knowledge that was valuable. The depth of experience they acquired made it possible for them to see things that a parent of a novice athlete might overlook.

In almost every interview we conducted, we asked people what advice they would give to parents of young athletes. What do they wish they had known when they were making initial decisions about what activities to sign up their kids for? In this chapter, we share those insights with you. First, we offer words of wisdom from seasoned parents of athletes. Most of those individuals had been overseeing their children's athletic careers for a decade or more. Next, we share the advice offered by youth sports coaches. Finally, we bring a new voice into the conversation—the college coach. Those coaches, who have experience working at all three NCAA levels, at schools spread across the country, could reflect on the long-term development of athletes that we found particularly interesting. The ideas shared by these three groups of adults confirm some of the points we made in previous chapters, but also highlight points that have not been raised before.

Parent Perspectives

All of the parents we spoke with initially signed up their kids to play for local recreational leagues—AYSO soccer, Little League Baseball/Softball, CYO basketball, and other nonprofit organizations. Their motivations for doing so were simple: to have fun, make friends, and get some exercise. Most parents looked back on that stage of their children's lives with a sense of fond nostalgia, but that honeymoon period did not last long.

In today's society, children may jump from recreational sports to more competitive leagues when they can still count their age on two hands. At that stage, things can get complicated. Decisions that seem inconsequential at the time can have long-term ramifications. It's possible that an athlete could end up playing for the same team for a decade or more. Parents who had been involved in youth sports for several years encouraged other mothers, fathers, and guardians to initiate discussions with children about their reasons for wanting to play sports. This seems like a straightforward piece of advice, but we discovered that parents rarely have those kinds of conversations with their kids.

They tend to make decisions based on what other people are doing rather than on what is best for their own children. It is especially important to have frank discussions before signing up a kid to play for a travel team.

"Make sure they like it," one parent advised. "Make sure they like the game and enjoy coming out here because it's an extra time commitment. Not only in time, because you've got that extra practice, but you're also traveling more. So they've got to be willing to commit to that." Children often notice the flashy parts of playing on a competitive team—the uniforms, the trophies, the opportunities to travel—without considering the sacrifices they will need to make to earn those rewards. How would they feel about missing a birthday party or summer camp if those events conflict with team commitments? Taking the time to gauge a child's level of interest is a worthwhile investment. As one mother remarked, "If your child is happy, if you're not forcing them to do something they don't want to do, they will have a positive experience."

Another step parents can take to increase the chances their kids will thrive is to gather information about the various options available to them before making decisions about teams or leagues. A parent's recollections about their own experiences as an athlete may no longer apply to the contemporary world of youth sports. The system is constantly evolving—and can be confusing. "I wish someone had told me about the whole structure so that we could've more actively made the choice to put [our son] on a travel team that was on his trajectory, that was their choice." Like many of the parents we interviewed, this mother let the system control her son's athletic development rather than actively deciding how sports fit into her child's life. This was not because the parent was negligent. She had thought a great deal about what kind of a person she hoped her son would become. Her knowledge of the youth sports industry, however, was limited. She didn't have a clear sense of the different levels of play or the demands associated with playing for an elite team.

The term "travel team" is applied to a wide range of clubs. As one mother explained, "You know travel team is a broad term. There are some travel teams that play locally, so you know you're going to nearby towns, but that's as far as you go, and the idea is to have a good time and there's not so much pressure. But other teams are worried about national rankings." Some travel teams are run by local towns, with limited time commitments and fees. Others fall under the umbrella term "pay-to-play." Pay-to-play clubs tend to cost more, travel further distances, and employ professional coaches. In both cases, a single organization may offer multiple teams for players of a certain age. Based on their performance at try outs, players could be placed on the A, B, C, or D team. They might be expected to play all-year-round or a season may last only a few months.

The parents we interviewed emphasized the importance of finding a team that matches the player's goals and level of commitment. According to one parent, "You don't necessarily have to join one of those fancy schmancy clubs to have a good experience." Another person observed that "Every travel team is not a perfect fit for every player. It's important to make sure it's the right fit. Pay attention to things like level of play and coaching style."

Some parents shared glowing reports of their children's coaches; others expressed more critical views. Both groups emphasized the powerful impact that coaches had on their kids' experiences with sports. Coaches have the power to inspire their players or to extinguish their interest in a sport. In recognition of this reality, parents advised adults who are thinking about signing up their kids to play on a travel team to learn about potential coaches before making decisions. Very few of the people we interviewed had done this themselves. It wasn't something they seriously considered. But many wished they had.

"You've got to get an idea of what the coach is like," one father related. "Talk to the coach to get a sense as to what the coach's philosophy is. Try to find out what the coach's goals are." Ask them about the team's practice schedule, how often they travel, and which tournaments they play in. Another dad shared the following advice: "Make sure you have a coach who has balance and is fair in their demands. Attend a game or a practice. Pay attention to the way the coach interacts with the players. How does he respond to players who make mistakes? How does she treat players on the bench?" At a practice or game, "You can actually see how the players interact with each other as well as seeing how the coach interacts with the players," one mother told us. "You know, there were some teams that we saw where the kids were really yelling and screaming at each other, which clearly was indicative of the fact that the coach was clearly always yelling and screaming at them."

Finally, some parents stressed that if a player no longer enjoys playing for a particular team, it might be a good idea to switch to a different organization. Within a system that often seems rigid from the outside, players do have some autonomy. They are not required to continue playing for the same team year after year. Shifts between clubs are more common than many parents realize. For example, during the period between elementary and middle school, kids often decide they no longer want to spend so much time playing sports. This creates openings on rosters that need to be filled. One parent told us about a young athlete who decided to leave their basketball team: "In talking to his mom, I remember she ended up being happier with where she landed, even though the process of having him leave the team was hard." Moving to a new team may seem daunting, but it can rekindle a player's interest in a sport.

Given the serious investments of time and money involved in youth sports today, it makes sense to think carefully before picking a team. The comments expressed by veteran sports parents underscored the benefits of making decisions with a focus on a child's social and physical development rather than on the prestige of potential teams. In other words, child-centered rather than league-driven parenting.

Travel Team Coaches

To get a sense of how the people who work most closely with young athletes approach their work, we interviewed dozens of coaches. Most of those adults were affiliated with travel teams, but we also spoke with individuals who coached recreation league teams. Most of them had been involved in youth sports for several years and had a wealth of experience to draw from. We were curious to hear their thoughts about the responsibilities of sports parents today.

One point of consensus among the coaches was that travel clubs have eclipsed recreational and scholastic leagues in terms of the influence they have on the youth sports industry. In most locations, interest in travel teams has expanded rapidly, at the expense of local nonprofit organizations like Little League and AYSO. In that environment, playing for a travel team may feel like an unavoidable necessity for many young athletes. As one coach who has coached at both levels remarked, "I tell parents who are on intramural, if you just want something for Suzy to do in the afternoon, then it's fine. But if you really want them to start growing, then you need to move to a travel team." Coaches also emphasized that travel teams vary considerably in terms of the expectations they place on players and their families. One travel team could compete against teams in the same county; another might fly to tournaments in other states. As families decide which teams to sign up for, they should think carefully about what they are hoping to get out of the experience.

According to the coaches, problems often surface as a result of clashes between parental expectations and team goals. As you might have guessed, those conflicts usually involve unrealistic plans established by ambitious parents. "My advice would be to let go," one coach told us. "Let go of the idea that your kid needs to be on the best team. But it's hard to let go of that because you never thought it would get so intense, and then suddenly you're in the middle of it. It's hard to keep a sense of perspective when it comes to your kids." Another coach advised parents to "Keep it simple. Resist the pressure to follow the lead of other parents."

Echoing the advice voiced by parents, several coaches encouraged families to learn as much as they can about potential teams before making any commitments. "The advice I would give," one person told us, "is to find out who the coach is and watch that coach on the sidelines. Find out what the coach's priorities are. Find out what the coach is hoping to accomplish in the next six weeks, in the next six months, in the next year, and see if that's something you're interested in pursuing." Interestingly, it was the coaches who expressed the most serious concerns about their peers. They all shared stories about opposing coaches whose behavior concerned them—people who screamed at players, challenged referees, or condoned bad sportsmanship. Those types of behavior are especially common among coaches whose salaries are paid by private companies.

The system is organized to encourage extreme actions. This can accelerate the development of talented players, but the costs can be significant. The higher the stakes, the more pervasive the questionable behavior of adults in leadership positions. As one coach explained, "They're being paid to get wins. . . . So therefore, they're furious when mistakes are being made." Another person noted that "These pay-to-play coaches put these big dreams in these kids' heads, and the only people who end up getting hurt are the kids, and that's what makes me sad." This concern for children being harmed by over-the-top/unethical/cutthroat coaches ran through our interviews. All the people we spoke with had witnessed offensive behavior firsthand. They had seen what a devastating impact it can have on young athletes.

It might surprise some parents to hear that many of the coaches we spoke with also shared their concerns about early specialization. They recognized playing a single sport year-round can damage a young athlete physically and mentally. Investing heavily in a single sport may seem to provide a young athlete with a competitive edge, coaches told us, but may ultimately have the opposite effect. "I really feel that what happens when these kids start young is that they get burned out too fast," a soccer coach told us. "You know, I've heard coaches tell their players when they're nine or ten, 'You have to make a commitment to this team and this team only.' But the kids I've watched grow up and play only soccer or baseball or hockey, whatever sport they chose, they only concentrate on that one sport, but they're done by ninth or tenth grade. They're just burnt out."

This advice about selecting a team may sound reasonable to parents, but what alternatives do they have? If their children decide not to specialize early, will they fall behind their peers? Will taking the idealistic route come back to bite them later? When we asked coaches about the idea that young athletes should focus on a single sport, they pushed back. According to one coach, "That's the one falsehood that gets promoted." To back up this statement, he described former players who specialized early and quit early with athletes who shifted smoothly from one sport to another. The variety of physical activities helped them develop skills that could be applied to multiple sports—without getting injured. Kids mature at different rates, coaches told us. How they perform at the age of eight does not determine what they will accomplish when they are eighteen. Their bodies and their interests change. Given this fact, it makes sense to follow their natural inclinations and interests. Make decisions based on what they want to do and be prepared to make adjustments. A sports psychologist we interviewed encouraged parents to "Focus on programs that emphasize development but are also fun for kids. It doesn't have to be extremely structured. It doesn't have to be every day of the week to benefit kids."

According to one coach, parent, and former semiprofessional athlete we interviewed, "At the end of the day, it is up to the child. We have to recognize that the child has their own brain. They're a human They have their own wants, needs, and desires, and if they want it, they'll work toward it. Teaching them work ethic. Teaching them to find a dream, find a passion and work toward it. That's what we should focus on. We should harness that and let them decide what they want to be in life."

College Coaches

Throughout this book, we have focused on the experiences of parents of athletes. In this section, we explore this topic from the perspective of college coaches and athletic directors. Although the purpose of this project was not to help parents get their children scholarships to play sports in the NCAA, we think college coaches have some valuable insights into the world of youth sports today. Their experiences—as, parents, coaches and administrators, and former players—give them a depth of knowledge that adds additional layers to the issues that anchor this book. You may be surprised by some of their views about contemporary youth sports.

We interviewed eight college coaches and three athletic directors. This group included people who have worked at colleges and universities located across the country, from Division I to Division III. All had witnessed major changes in the youth sports industry and had been forced to adjust to that transformation. The growth of travel sports has had a particularly powerful impact on their interactions with potential recruits. Coaches told us that an athlete's performance on her high school team means very little to them. "In the old days," a soccer coach explained, "you'd always go to high school games. But with the expansion of club sports, you go to the club sports programs. If a kid is exceptional at high school that really doesn't mean a lot to us. So it's critical that players play outside of high school and play in a club sports program."

Several of the coaches expressed concerns about the effects that commercialization of the industry has had on young athletes. Even the critics, though, acknowledged that to get recognized by college recruiters, high school athletes need to play for teams that participate in regional tournaments and showcases. According to a basketball coach, "It's really sad, but when a kid tells me that they don't participate in a clubs sport, or that they're not on an AAU team, I kind of think about it in the sense that, how serious are they about their sport?" That is true for athletes interested in playing at the Division I level as well as those with an eye on Division III programs.

Although the college coaches all recognized the importance of playing for a travel team, they also cautioned parents to proceed slowly and cautiously. As an athletic director explained, "One thing I have learned about being a coach in athletics and sports is that, developmentally, you can't tell what a ten-year-old is going to be like when they're seventeen or eighteen, because of their maturation." She went on to share the experiences of her own daughter, who, as a college sophomore, asked her, "Mom, whatever happened to all of those girls that played travel soccer? They were going to play Division I soccer." I said, 'Honey, they moved on.' We only knew two who played soccer in college. We never heard from any of those others." From the perspective of this athletic director, an athlete's performance at age ten means very little.

Most of the college coaches we talked to shared similar stories. Their observations suggested that many parents do not have a thorough understanding of the recruiting process. They tend to make decisions based on rumors they hear from other parents or their gut instincts. When that is the case, the results can be disappointing for everyone involved. Young athletes need advocates—adults who look out for and protect them. But a misguided advocate can create problems for the people they are trying to help.

All of the coaches we interviewed had worked with athletes whose ambitions clashed with reality. In most cases, the parents were responsible for nurturing those unrealistic dreams. "I think parents ruin it for their kids," related a women's basketball coach. "They are feeding information to their kids that isn't necessarily true, whether it's how good they are, how much they should be playing, or just being way too involved." According to college coaches, one of the most common mistakes parents make is to make decisions about potential colleges based on unrealistic expectations. They assume, because their son excelled on his travel club or high school team, he will succeed at the college level. That is not always the case.

Steady expansion of travel sports over the past twenty-five years has created opportunities for almost any young athlete to play for a team that someone considers "elite." It has also nurtured the ambitious of parents who want to believe their kids are exceptional. However, as we document in Chapter Four (Scholarship Dreams), the number of spots on college team rosters has not increased. The percentage of high school athletes who make it to the NCAA is quite small—approximately one in thirteen high school athletes go on to play a varsity sport in college and one in fifty-seven make it to a Division I program. Those odds have not registered with many parents of athletes.

According to one college coach, the most common misconception parents have about collegiate athletics is that "they're all going to get Division I scholarships." They also tend to have unrealistic expectations about playing time and the demands placed on student athletes. When parents become convinced their prepubescent child is destined to play Division I sports, that sense of certainty can cloud their judgment. As a men's soccer coach lamented, "The intensity of pressure on the kids is wrong. And the pressure oftentimes, not always but oftentimes, comes from the parents." A women's soccer coach voiced a similar concern: "We're creating a situation in those types of things that are unhealthy for our youth. We're forcing a twelve-year-old to make a decision about which team they want to choose, and feeding them all kinds of information, and they're not equipped to make those decisions. We're putting them in uncomfortable positions a lot of times, and I don't think that's the purpose of youth sports."

How can parents apply this information as they make decisions for their kids? The advice from college coaches seems contradictory. On the one hand, they state that if an athlete wants to compete at the college level, she should play on a travel team and participate in high-profile tournaments; on the other hand, they assert that parents put too much pressure on their kids. These kinds of mixed messages can be confusing to parents, especially those with limited sports-related experience.

Commercialization of the youth sports industry has spurred changes that are not good for athletes or the people responsible for mentoring them. The system, coaches indicated, is not going to change anytime soon. However, college coaches also shared ideas about how families can negotiate a flawed system. Their observations point to some concrete steps parents can take to increase their children's chances of having fulfilling athletic careers.

One most important takeaway from the college coaches is that while kids who aspire to play at the college level will need to join a competitive travel team at some point—that decision should be delayed until the athlete is physically and psychologically mature. Coaches as well as athletic directors emphasized the benefits of playing multiple sports before specializing in one. As an athletic director explained, "They need to be exposed. If you have the resources, expose your kid to playing ice hockey or volleyball or tennis, or whatever. One sport is going to help the other." In other words, different sports require athletes to develop different muscles. Shifting from one sport to another also reduces the chances that an athlete will suffer from over-use injuries. It also reduces the chances they will burn out.

Every coach and athletic director we interviewed recalled players they had worked with who succeeded in getting recruited to play sports at the NCAA level, but lost their interest in a sport soon after entering college. One person, for example, recalled that "A lot of student-athletes are burnt out by the time they get to college. I've had a lot of my softball players say, 'I don't want to play anymore. I've had too much of this. This is all I've ever done and now I want to have fun.'" That decision marked the end of her softball career. A woman's soccer coach told us about a player she had recruited for her team didn't make it through her first college season. Midway through that season she informed the coach, "I don't want to play anymore. My parents forced me to play."

To avert that type of crash, parents should avoid putting unnecessary pressure on their kids. Make decisions based on which team is the best match for their child rather than on club ranking. It is important to consider the demands that will be placed on the player, the type of coaching they will receive, and how the team fits into their life as a student. As one coach remarked, "I think the biggest thing is to understand that this is not an investment in your child's future. People look at it that way. When you start attaching words like 'investment' to an extracurricular activity, that creates so many expectations that are unfair for the students. Look at it for what it is: an opportunity to participate in athletics, to better yourself as a person."

Coaches advised parents to set realistic expectations. Be open to the possibility that a kid who loves playing basketball when they're eight-years-old may decide to switch to swimming just a few years later. Try to create space so that a child has the freedom to make those shifts.

Advice from the Field

Over the last few years, we spoke with countless people connected to the world of youth sports. The stories they told us were gripping, concerning, enlightening, inspiring—almost any adjective you can think of. We always asked people to share any advice they would give to parents of young athletes. In this chapter, we have presented those words of wisdom. As might be expected, the parents, travel team coaches, and people working in NCAA athletics held a wide range of opinions. Some of the comments they shared contradicted ideas expressed by others. That is not surprising, given their diverse backgrounds. However, there were some common themes to the comments they made, which we will highlight here:

- If they are truly invested in their children's development as athletes, parents need to do their homework before making important decisions. Simply following the lead of friends and neighbors may be easier, but it can also lead parents to make decisions they later regret. To avoid this trap, take the time to learn as much as possible about potential coaches and teams. Informed consumers make better decisions than those who rely on advertisements.

• Avoid the temptation to have your children specialize in a single sport until they are physically mature and emotionally prepared to make that commitment. Specializing may ultimately make sense—but not before athletes have finished elementary school. Playing multiple sports will help them develop a wide range of skills without putting unnecessary stress on their bodies.

• The world of youth sports has become increasingly intense and stressful for everyone involved. Parents are required to dedicate significant amounts of time and money to their children's athletic activities. This makes it easy to lose a sense of perspective. When faced with difficult decisions, step back, talk to your kid, and try to keep the child's needs at the center—not your own.

• Children learn all sorts of things through participating in sports. They develop physically, socially, and emotionally. As kids mature and engage in higher levels of competition, it's important to remember the reason they wanted to play sports in the first place: to have fun. If a kid no longer enjoys playing a sport, it is probably time to move on to a different activity or a new team.

In our society today, resisting pressure to do whatever it takes to make your child stand out from the pack can be difficult. Parents are constantly bombarded with messages that lead them to question the decisions they make for their kids. Raising children can feel like a competition. When adults choose to join that contest without thinking through the consequences, their children often suffer. We found the following advice from a college soccer coach particularly helpful:

> Every year, I meet a new parent, and I tell them that the moment they look into the crib of their baby that they're not going to be on the National Team or be President of the United States, everything is so much easier. Because as a parent, you believe your kid is going to do this, this, and this, and everything else, but the moment you settle down and just recognize that it might not happen, the parents become that much better in terms of supporting and helping the kid in an appropriate way, instead of pushing them.

This statement underscores an idea voiced by the parents, coaches, and athletic directors we interviewed—the importance of supporting rather than pushing young athletes. We agree.

CHAPTER ELEVEN

Conclusion

"I would probably warn [parents] about the folks that are just going to tell them what they want to hear. They'll talk up their program. . . . They'll take your money, these guys will definitely take your money. . . . But that doesn't mean you shouldn't go and pursue a club team, it's just which one you pick, how much money you spend on it, you know, how realistic you are."

— Youth sports parent —

"What drives me is the opportunity to offer these kids some life lessons as they translate into adulthood, and things that they'll carry with them for life. For me, it's kind of an opportunity to give back to something that I enjoyed growing up myself."

— Youth baseball coach —

The research we have presented in this book highlights many ambiguities, complexities, and conundrums related to the roles parents play in their children's athletic careers. One finding, however, is clear: the world of sports has undergone extensive changes over a relatively short period of time. When parents today reflect on their experiences playing sports as children, those images are likely to look remarkably different from what they see today. Memories of riding their bikes with other kids in the neighborhood to the local ball field to play a ball game may produce warm feelings of nostalgia, but they are also anachronistic. More likely, their own children are driven to practices that take place several miles from home. Those practices are probably monitored by groups of parents eager to see how their sons or daughters compare with other players. And there is a good chance that by the time their children hit their teens, they will start playing sports year-round, competing in tournaments organized to showcase talented athletes.

The rapid intensification of youth sports that we have described in this book could be viewed as positive or negative, depending on your values and goals. Parents we interviewed often lamented that sports exerted an outsized influence on their sons and daughters; that athletic practices and games dominated their lives. But beneath that surface level expression of dissatisfaction, parents frequently conveyed support for activities they seemed to condemn. Fathers who complained about the long hours demanded of young athletes signed up their children for optional training sessions or ID camps. Mothers who shook their heads while listing the costs associated with playing on a travel team bought their kids top-of-the-line basketball sneakers, warm-up suits, or bats. Very few opted out of the system, which is always an option.

A parent or coach could argue that the extensive demands placed on young athletes today help them develop their abilities to an extent that wasn't common only a few years ago. As our society has boosted its emphasis on youth sports, the resources dedicated to training, coaching, and monitoring the development of athletes have also increased. Although it's difficult to compare practices across generations, it does seem as though the quality of coaching today is generally higher than was the case a generation ago. In the past, most coaches were parents with limited expertise in the sports they oversaw. Today, college coaches and professional trainers work with athletes who have yet to graduate from elementary school. When we were kids, few adults would have contemplated paying a private coach to videotape their child swinging a bat, analyze that film, and put together a detailed plan for improvement. Today, hundreds of companies offer those services.

This type of concentrated attention to sports appears to have elevated the level of performance demonstrated by our youth. Should we celebrate that development? Are the larger investments families are making producing greater dividends? Some parents believe the pressures experienced by young athletes have spiraled out of control and are damaging young bodies and minds. Others appreciate the expanded opportunities that are now provided to their talented offspring; access to elite coaching has given their sons and daughters the skills that could lead to careers in the NCAA. That might not have been possible if they played a sport for only three or four months of the year, coached by generous but inexperienced parent volunteers.

Regardless of your views of the current system, one clear and indisputable finding of our research is that parents are struggling to keep abreast of the constantly evolving world of youth sports. Overseeing the athletic activities of their sons and daughters has become complicated and stressful. Just when parents think they finally understand how the system works, a new league sprouts up and invites their child to try out, or they are told they should really consider signing up for a specialized summer camp. Well-intentioned parents try their best to help their children succeed, but the metrics for measuring success are constantly shifting. This uncertainty can make it incredibly difficult for them to make sound decisions.

Reflections on Changes in the Youth Sports Industry

When reporters comment on youth sports, they tend to frame their observations as if adults make decisions rationally, after carefully evaluating the impact those decisions have on their children.

Those articles often assign success or blame to individuals, when multiple factors are actually involved. They can also oversimplify complex situations. Simplicity can be reassuring, especially when emotions are involved. If we are convinced that our team lost a critical match due to errors made by the coach or referee, directing our emotions at that individual can feel cathartic. If only that person had put a particular player in the game or made the right call in a critical situation, our team could have won.

This way of thinking can create a sense of clarity in our minds, for simplistic assessments yield simplistic solutions: If we could just crack down on the behavior of individuals, our problems would be solved. This helps to explain why criticism of youth sports so often focuses on the actions of the "unhinged sports parent." When we interviewed sports parents, they often talked about the problematic behavior of adult participants (coaches and other parents). If someone could control those individuals, they implied, our problems would fade away.

But our research suggests that the situation is much more complicated. As we analyzed our interviews with players and adults, observation notes taken at athletic events, and survey data, we concluded that a number of developments occurring over the past twenty-five years have combined to reshape the youth sports landscape. We did observe some adults who behaved inappropriately, who struggled to maintain their composure in tense situations. But those types of transgressions have always occurred at sporting events. If you are not persuaded by this observation, watch *The Bad News Bears* one more time. Parents have always struggled to control their emotions at athletic events.

We are convinced that changes in common perceptions of youth sports are the result of a confluence of factors linked to broader shifts in culture, economics, communication, and business. These shifts magnify the significance of individual actions and misdirect public concerns about the role that sports currently plays in the lives of children. Rather than focus on extreme actions of individuals, it would be beneficial to pay closer attention to forces that lead to problematic behavior.

Factor One: Rapid Changes in the Industry

For parents who grew up when community sports leagues were the norm, the current sprawling industry that surrounds youth athletics can feel overwhelming. What was once a fairly simple and straightforward system seems to spawn additional layers every year. It's as if a two-dimensional chessboard developed a third layer, and players must learn to navigate the new game without receiving an updated set of rules.

When their children first started playing organized sports, it may have appeared that little has changed in recent years. Parents of young athletes still sign up their sons and daughters to play on a community-based team. Commitments are minimal and player development is emphasized. But this introductory phase can be short-lived. Only a year or two after playing on their first recreational team, a young athlete might be invited to try out for a travel team that competes against clubs from other cities. Ten or fifteen years ago, this option was not generally offered to athletes until they had entered adolescence and had demonstrated over a period of years that they were unusually gifted.

Today, children may feel pressure to try out for travel teams before their ages reach double-digits. At this stage in a young athlete's life, it is difficult to determine a child's athletic potential or the depth of their interest in a particular sport. For this reason, many sports psychologists recommend against specializing in a particular sport until the age of thirteen or fourteen.[38] Instead, children are advised to participate in a variety of activities to keep their bodies flexible and to prevent burnout at a young age.

Following that advice, however, can be difficult. The allure of playing for a travel team can seem glamorous for impressionable young athletes—and their parents. Why limit yourself to the AYSO soccer team when you have an opportunity to play for a club that competes in tournaments in other cities and states? Wearing a travel team jacket to school can seem infinitely more enticing than a piece of clothing adorned with the name of the local car dealership or pharmacy that sponsors a town team.

And this hierarchy of sports status becomes more complex as one gets older. The definition of elite seems difficult to decipher and constantly under revision. Within a single town, there may be multiple travel teams that divide talented athletes according to their perceived ability, often based on performance at a brief tryout session. In addition, players might be invited to audition for regional teams or "pay-to-play" clubs that claim to prepare their players for success at the highest levels of competitive sports. The aspirational ladder for ambitious young athletes seems to have no upper rung.

For parents who grew up just twenty or thirty years ago, making sense of the youth sports industry can feel like a losing battle. What level of competition is most appropriate for their child? How much money should they invest in their athletic career? What are the benefits of committing to a club that plays year-round, and what are the downsides? These are all important questions for parents to consider; answering them requires parents to do some detective work, for the answers are not always clear or easily accessible.

The combination of a rapidly evolving youth sports industry and the dearth of dependable information about travel clubs puts many parents in a bind. Lacking a clear understanding of where their children fit into this convoluted web of sports activities, parents tend to follow the lead of their friends. When confronted with uncertainty, adults often choose the path of least resistance. Personal connections trump all other considerations. For young children, this approach makes sense, given their social and physical immaturity. But as players advance through the system and their bodies mature at different rates, unquestioningly following the lead of other parents is not always in a young athlete's best interests.

Expansion of the youth sports industry has influenced the decisions made by parents in another way. As the choices parents must make have become more convoluted, the pressure to increase their investments in their children's athletic careers has intensified. Opting for anything less than the highest level team, summer camp, or training program can be a difficult decision for any parent to make. And the longer a child continues to play competitive sports, the stronger the push to go all-in becomes. During our period of research, we encountered very few parents who made a conscious decision to reduce the intensity of their children's sports activities over time. As the stakes increased, so too did the size of their investments.

Factor Two: Inflated Dreams

For most of the previous century, playing sports was seen as an end in itself. Children organized games in the street, signed up for a local league, or played for their school team because it was fun. Earning a varsity letter might have elevated a student's status among his peers, but only exceptional athletes planned to continue their sports careers after graduating from high school. That started to change in the 1990s, when travel sports leagues began to proliferate.

As we have noted, the volume of clubs that served talented young athletes expanded rapidly. Such growth impelled changes in both the structure of youth sports leagues and popular conceptions of athletic excellence. Earning awards based on an outstanding high school career no longer separated outstanding athletes from the rest of the pack. To truly distinguish themselves, they needed to advance to higher and higher levels of the sports hierarchy. As that mindset became widespread, the number of young athletes intent on playing sports year-round skyrocketed. Not surprisingly, adult entrepreneurs formed new teams, leagues, and businesses to meet the demand. It is important to recognize the number of slots on high school and college teams remained fairly steady over this period of expansion. Yet the volume of children who signed up to play on elite teams continued to grow.

That development would not be problematic if families had realistic expectations about their children's athletic futures. But travel sports teams no longer serve only extraordinarily gifted individuals. Even an average athlete can find a spot on a club that plays year-round if she is motivated. Yet the perception that club sports groom players to play at the college level has endured. As a result, parents explicitly or inadvertently nurture the dreams of young athletes who might not have a realistic shot at advancing to the college level. The sheer volume of adolescents who participate in travel sports means that large numbers of kids come to believe they have a chance to play softball at UCLA or basketball for Michigan State. In actuality, fewer than 2 percent of high school athletes eventually play NCAA Division I sports.

This mismatch between perception and reality is exacerbated by a couple of factors. First, because families commit to travel sports when their children are much younger than was true a generation ago, the amount of time and money they invest in their children's athletic careers can be substantial. If an athlete starts playing on a travel team when he is eight years old, his parents could spend close to $20,000 on athletics by the time their child graduates from high school. Families make other, nonfinancial investments in athletics as well. Parents devote countless hours driving their children to practices, games, and tournaments; they miss out on social events and vacations; and the psychic energy investments in a child's athletic career can be considerable.

When parents make such significant investments in a child's sports career, many expect to receive some sort of payout in the future. Given the considerable commitment they have made to sports over a number of years, it only seems fair that their child should have the opportunity to continue playing after high school. The countless hours of intense training and competitive tournaments, they believe, have prepared her to succeed at the college level. This reasoning is likely to make sense especially for parents who went to school at a time when only truly exceptional athletes played on travel teams. Why else would college scouts be lined up, clipboards in hand, at the showcase tournaments their children compete in? Numerous emails inviting them to participate in summer ID camps at colleges seem to confirm these parents' assumptions.

In this way, what has become a lucrative youth sports industry feeds, and often distorts, parents' hopes for their children. Those dreams are nurtured by an army of consultants eager to profit from young athletes and their parents. Private sports clubs, personal trainers, marketing experts, videographers, personal advisers, summer camp administrators, and coaches all have good reasons for feeding parental optimism. Financial considerations drive the behavior of most of these sports professionals. Convincing adults that the dreams they hold for the sons and daughters can be achieved—with sufficient commitment, training, and promotion—increase profit margins for youth sports businesses.

In sum, nurturing the aspirations of young athletes and their parents is in the best interests of a variety of people who profit from the youth sports industry. As the industry has grown, the volume and intensity of messages conveyed to parents have also increased. Parents are bombarded with information encouraging them to enroll their children in specialized conditioning programs, sign them up to play in the summer ID camps, or pay a videographer to compose a polished highlight film that can be sent to college scouts. Declining those offers can be difficult. In a system that constantly suggests your child has the potential to become a college sports star, maintaining a sense of equilibrium can prove daunting to even the most level-headed parent.

Factor Three: The Influence of Community
Although their initial motivations for becoming involved in youth sports are usually tied to their children's interests, the longer parents remain connected to those activities, the more they come to rely on other sports parents for support. At a very basic level, they depend on other adults to help with the logistical tasks associated with competitive sports. Sharing responsibility for driving kids to practices, attending meetings,

and chaperoning players at tournaments reduces the amount of time parents must devote to travel sports each week.

What may begin as a minimal time commitment can quickly develop into a central focus for both players and their family members. As their children get older, the amount of time parents spend with other travel team families steadily increases. Watching practices, staffing concession stands, and attending out-of-town tournaments creates opportunities for them to get to know other parents intimately. Those relationships can fortify their sense of belonging to a community of like-minded adults. For many of the parents we interviewed, sports created a sort of social glue, connecting them to parents with similar interests.

As we discuss in Chapter Five (The Mobile Neighborhood), the connections that develop among sports parents are tied to broader social and demographic changes. Geographical neighborhoods no longer serve as a form of social anchor for families in the way they once did. Adults may not know the names of the people who live on their street, let alone feel a strong affinity to them. This erosion of neighborhood cohesion has left a void in the lives of families around the country. Our interviews suggest that for parents of competitive athletes, the travel team community can serve as a mobile neighborhood that fills that gap. During their regularly scheduled interactions with other team families, they share stories, seek advice, and provide each other with emotional support.

The communities that form among parents can also reinforce some of the problematic aspects of contemporary youth sports culture. As their sports-related commitments increase, parents' social worlds tend to contract. The adults they come in contact most regularly are other mothers and fathers who are also devoted to their children's athletic careers. They are constantly surrounded by people who also have faith in the long-term benefits of sports specialization. This can create an echo chamber among adults involved in travel team sports.

Physical neighborhoods are often composed of people with diverse backgrounds and perspectives. In those settings, a parent might chat with adults who raise questions about the wisdom of focusing so much attention on youth sports. Among a group of adults who have invested considerable time and money in their children's athletic careers, on the other hand, the chances that someone will voice criticism of travel sports are minimal. As is the case of our Facebook or Instagram feeds, the messages we receive usually confirm our existing worldviews. Travel team parents may complain about a bad call at a game, the price of a tournament hotel, or a taxing practice schedule, but they are generally supportive of the entire enterprise. In this context, critical perspectives are unlikely to penetrate the protective wall that encases the travel team community.

For many parents today, maintaining a sense of balance between a child's extracurricular life and their own interests can be quite challenging. It is easy—almost natural—to set your own needs aside so that you can concentrate on your child's athletic accomplishments. Some of the parents we interviewed maintained clear distinctions between these two worlds, making sure to participate in activities that did not involve their children. More often, though, the mobile sports neighborhood gradually came to dominate their social lives. Similar to their children, parents attached greater weight to team-related activities as their commitments to the team grew. Sports activities began to dominate their time, relationships, and priorities.

In this way, performing the role of the sports parent became essential to their own sense of self. Their children's athletic accomplishments determined their own feelings of success or failure as parents. When their children graduated from high school or stopped playing sports, sports parents often struggled to fill the substantial void that was created. Although all parents go through a period of adjustment when their children leave home, this process was especially destabilizing for sports parents who became distanced not only from their children but also from the mobile neighborhoods that had anchored their lives for a number of years.

The phenomena we have described is not limited to the world of youth sports. Rather, it reflects broader changes that shape the social lives of adults and children today. We would expect, for example, to observe similar behavior among parents of aspiring professional dancers. As their children become more serious about dancing, they could very well develop a sense of insularity and tunnel vision. Parents of dancers accepted into the training program for the Joffrey Ballet would be more likely to trade advice about how to increase their chances of making it to the upper levels of the ballet world than to encourage another parent to take a more relaxed approach to ballet. As is the case with sports, dance organizations prey on the insecurities of ballet parents. When we consulted the Joffrey website, an advertisement for "Summer Intensive" training programs offered in twelve cities immediately popped up. We recognized the familiar encouragement to "Register today before it is too late!" with the anxiety-inducing reminder that "Spots are filling in quickly!"

In sports as well as the arts, our social worlds are becoming narrower and more intense. The bonds that form among parents involved in any activity that places significant demands on them can provide stability in their lives and can also encourage them to do whatever it takes to help their child get ahead. In a society that increasingly values surface level connections that require minimal face-to-face contact, competitive sports can help facilitate dependable interactions among like-minded parents. Yet while those relationships may offer sports parents a sense of belonging and support, they may also undermine their ability to make sound decisions for their kids.

Beyond a Culture of Competition

Sports are inherently competitive, typically organized around contests with teams vying to win. For most elite athletes, especially those who earn a living from playing sports, winning is certainly the primary goal. Professional and major college coaches' jobs depend on winning and players are routinely evaluated on their contributions to winning games, leagues, and championships. Perhaps it is no surprise the youth sports industry, with the rising visibility of national and regional rankings for youth sports teams and the growth of so-called "national" tournaments, has become increasingly focused on winning championships.

At the same time, youth sports are competitive in another, more individualized way. That is, players compete with each other, even their own teammates, for recognition, attention, playing time, and the opportunity to play at the next level. While many high schools tout their history of state championships, including those from decades past, with prominent signs on town highways and banners hanging from high school gymnasiums, high-profile travel programs are more likely to promote their success with announcements of player commitments to play at a particular college rather than team victories. For many parents of aspiring athletes, especially when considering a travel team that costs many thousands of dollars a year, a demonstrated record of successfully placing travel team players on collegiate rosters is a more important measuring stick than is the number of recent tournament championships.

The paradox that youth sports, still often hyper-focused on winning on game day, has become increasingly organized around individual accomplishment over team success may be best illustrated by college "showcase" events, where highly competitive travel teams attend tournaments to showcase the abilities of their individual players for college coaches who attend to observe aspiring collegiate players. In showcase tournaments, the "winners" are those whose performance garners the attention of college recruiters. In this competition, the most sought after prize is not the tournament trophy but an invitation to visit a college campus. And so it goes. In this era of often-intense competition among individual young athletes, it is rare to see information about team success on players' recruiting profile sites, where individual accomplishments and performance metrics are the principal currency.

Individual athletic success, of course, always coexists with failure, as anyone who has played competitive sports can attest. It is no exaggeration to say that all athletes, from elite-level professionals to young children, have had the experience of making mistakes, performing poorly in a pivotal moment, or losing a game. Failure is, in fact, an integral component of competitive sports. At a time of substantial public concern that contemporary youth are more anxious and fragile than previous generations,[39] we might look to youth sports as one site for thinking productively about the meaning and sources of resilience. Among the many parents who discussed the life lessons they hope their children would learn from playing sports, offering young athletes regular opportunities to learn from experiences of failure was the most prominent.

While high school age athletes may be focused on their own individual athletic careers, particularly as they near an inflection point that will, for most, mean an end to their time playing competitive sports, there are plenty of parents concerned that the youngest athletes will be turned off by the excesses of an ultra-competitive youth sports scene. In programs for players just getting started, coaches and parents often try to shift attention away from winning and losing, seeking to emphasize learning and fun. For many adults hoping to make sports fun and inviting for all kids, there is no reason to burden a five-year-old player with concerns about individual or team performance. Instead, adults sometimes collaborate to end games in a tie or decide not to keep score of games or track win-loss records. For most adults seeking to mitigate a focus on winning, their concern is that youth sports have come to imitate professional sports in a way that narrows the experience for young players. The goal is to open a window for young children to enjoy the experience of playing sports, being part of a team, and learning new skills before a culture of competition shifts the attention of players and parents alike to winning and achievement.

There is no getting around the fact that team sports is a fundamentally competitive enterprise. One team wins and another team loses. Some players perform well and others are less successful. That is all part of the game. But, as we have argued, youth sports is about more than just the game. While virtually every parent we talked with was laser focused on their own child's experience, the point of that focus was, for most parents, their child's happiness. Often, this was defined in relation to the team's winning (or, in the negative, team losing, since persistent losing is perceived by many parents to produce unhappy players). In addition, parents considered their children's happiness in relation to whether they had sufficient opportunity to play in games and whether the players performed at a sufficiently high level. Winning, playing time, and performance—each of these have deep roots in a culture of competition.

While competition may be what's most visible—every fan in the stands knows who won the game and can readily see who made the big shot or scored the key goal—youth sports can offer a far more expansive and dynamic experience. Community, care, and resilience coexist with competition as defining features of youth sport. The world of youth sports contains a richness that is rarely recognized: emphasizing competition as well as community, celebrating both accomplishment and connection, recognizing both the joy of victory and resilience in the face of failure. Perhaps it is precisely this multifaceted nature of youth sports that brings so many parents and children to the playing field and gymnasium each year.

Competition is the public face of youth sports. And for good reason. It is the central organizing principle of the youth sports industry. Nevertheless, a significant portion of participants, including many who wholeheartedly embrace a culture of competition, see something more in youth sports: a road to friendship and social connection, experiencing the joy of teamwork, physical activity that can be both healthy and fun, the opportunity to learn about one's own body, and a powerful arena for young people to develop resilience. While an overemphasis on competition and achievement can overshadow other ways of experiencing youth sports, it is important to recognize the range of possibilities that often hover just below the surface of our shared conversations about what parents and children might find within the world of youth sports.

Looking Forward

As we began this project, we had a general sense of the world of youth sports, but our views were largely informed by personal experience. When our children first joined travel sports teams, we, like most parents, were entering unfamiliar territory. Trying out for a travel team was what local kids were doing, and we followed the crowd. Over the years, we became more familiar with the ins and outs of the youth sports business.

During our children's many years of playing sports, we regularly spent weekends talking with other parents on the sidelines, sharing rides to practices, games, and tournaments, and listening as parents described their aspirations for their children. Our experiences volunteering as travel team coaches and local league administrators gave us a broader perspective. In managing a team or helping to operate a youth sports program, we got a close-up view behind the scenes, and observed the challenges of recruiting and retaining participants, the economic dynamics of the expanding youth sports industry, and the kinds of expectations so many young athletes face. We discovered the importance that parents attach to their children's athletic accomplishments tends to increase as their children advance through the system. The escalation of demands placed on athletes and their families can cause parents to make decisions that are not in their children's best interests. Surrounded by people who prioritize performance over development, they lose their sense of perspective.

The sheer volume of messages that parents of developing athletes receive can create a sense of information overload. Among the parents we interviewed and observed, the most common response to that situation was to follow the lead of other parents, who were rarely better informed than they were. Parents tended to make decisions based on intuition, hearsay, and blind faith. That tendency fed the very beast that was preying upon their sons and daughters. Uninformed consumers make excellent customers. When faced with uncertainty, parents tend to take the path of least resistance. In the world of youth sports, this involves signing up children for more demanding, time consuming, and expensive activities.

So what can be done to address this situation? Given the emphasis we have placed on the unbridled expansion of youth sports industry that has taken place recently, it might seem logical for us to advocate for an overhaul of the industry. Reducing the influence of private business on youth sports could restore the more relaxed, low-key aspects of athletics that we remember fondly from our youth. Keeping money out of youth sports would reduce the demands placed on youth athletes and their families.

However, although we do recognize the problems that commercialization of the youth sports industry has created, we also understand that revamping the system would be an enormous undertaking. The business interests that profit from the youth sports market have become deeply entrenched. They are also decentralized; no single company or organization controls the multitude of sports-related businesses that operate today. Tackling the most problematic aspects of this enterprise extends beyond the capabilities of the average parent.

For this reason, we advocate more child-specific responses to the issues highlighted in this book. Parents may not have the resources required to change the behavior of large corporations, but they can influence the people and organizations that more directly shape youth sports in their communities. Putting pressure on local clubs to more actively monitor the behavior of adults could reduce cases of unruly behavior on and around athletic fields. Organizations like the Positive Coaching Alliance (PCA), for example, provide training workshops to parents, coaches, and schools around the country. The PCA subscribes to the view that "learning to treat people with dignity, especially under the pressure of competition, is one of the most valuable life lessons sports can offer."[40] We fully support this way of framing sports for children and have seen how groups like the PCA have given parents concrete strategies for reducing the pressures experienced by their sons and daughters.

On a more immediate level, parents can give more thought to the long-term goals they have for their children and make decisions with careful attention to those objectives. What do they ultimately hope their sons and daughters will get out of participating in sports? Many would assume that if talented athletes are going to have successful careers in sports, they must commit fully to athletics. After all, many of our sports heroes committed to year-round training and intense competition from a young age. If they hadn't adopted such single-minded devotion to sports, they might not have made it to the professional ranks.

While we recognize there is some truth to that last statement, we also know the vast majority of individuals who display athletic potential at a young age never play sports at the college or professional levels. And many of the professional athletes we celebrate did not become serious about sports until their teenage years. Michael Jordan did not make the varsity basketball team at his high school until his junior year, and then he became so burned out by professional basketball at one point that he retired and played minor league baseball.

We encourage parents to operate under the assumption that their children can lead very rewarding lives without letting sports dominate their daily lives. Rather than let sports dreams guide the decisions they make, parents could view athletic accomplishment as one of many possible indications of success. If their daughter ends up playing softball at the University of Arizona, that will be worth celebrating; but she might find just as much personal satisfaction if she decides to choose a college based on her academic goals and play softball at the intramural level. We interviewed many college students who played sports competitively as adolescents but decided to focus on other activities in college; none of those former athletes regretted that decision. Not a single one.

Taking such a holistic approach to youth sports may sound quite unrealistic. We admit that maintaining a long-term perspective on a child's development can be challenging. Given the problematic aspects of competitive athletics, it might make sense for some children to shift gears, quit competitive athletics, and focus on less-stressful activities. We can see why parents might think this makes sense for their children. But we also came across many parents who signed up their sons and daughters for competitive sports leagues and maintained a healthy perspective on the advantages and disadvantages of those commitments.

Our research suggests that the essential ingredient in this endeavor is *balance*. Rather than offer a formula that can be followed to ensure a young athlete succeeds, we encourage parents to make decisions that create balance in their children's lives. Kids who participate in a variety of activities, interact with all sorts of people, and have a chance to relax and decompress on a regular basis are more likely to thrive. The specific activities that children participate in will vary according to individual interests and may change over time. Encouraging kids to sample different pursuits and recognizing that failure is an inevitable part of growing up will help create balance in the lives of young athletes and their families. Children who take part in a variety of activities are more likely to bounce back from defeat than those whose lives are dominated by a single interest.

Following the advice offered by the parents and coaches in Chapter Ten can help to create balance in the lives of athletes and their families. The recommendations they shared acknowledge the realities of the current youth sports industry and also consider the role that athletics can—and should—play in an individual's social and emotional development. The consensus among experienced sports parents and coaches was that delaying specialization ultimately benefits athletes. Until they mature, physically and emotionally, children should be encouraged to play a variety of sports.

People might assume this approach would undermine the team's success, but most of the coaches we interviewed disagreed. As a veteran soccer coach told us, "I truly believe our kids playing other sports has led to our success on the soccer field, because when they come to play soccer, they're so psyched up to be playing . . . they might have missed a practice this week because they had a track meet, and you know there was a whole group of them, because indoor track and basketball started, that didn't come to practice. I have to say, in our tournament those kids stood out on the field because they were just stoked, so pumped and ready to play because they hadn't played soccer all week."

We recognize that many coaches are more interested in winning than in creating balance in children's lives. It may take some effort to find more accommodating mentors, but they do exist. Parents who uncritically follow the lead of other adults in their orbit might overlook coaches who could potentially inspire their children without putting enormous pressure on them. To avoid this trap, parents should think carefully about the qualities of a coach they most value and make decisions based on their goals and values.

Interestingly, when we asked parents what they hoped their children would learn through sports, they mentioned the value of life lessons more often than winning. Those lessons included things like persistence, the ability to work with others, overcoming adversity, and time management. Although almost everyone we interviewed valued those lessons, not all backed up their words with action. When an invitation to an elite summer camp or to try out for a highly ranked team, they found it difficult to resist those opportunities, even if they created additional stress for their children. If parents of young athletes follow the advice of the coach above and seek out coaches who emphasize life lessons over rankings or college connections, they are likely to create a solid foundation for their children's athletic—and personal—development.

The most well-adjusted athletes we observed invested time and energy in sports, but also participated in other extracurricular activities. Parents of these well-rounded young women and men resisted pressure to make decisions based on the assumption that their children would one day receive offers to play at the college level. Regarding a college athletic scholarship as one of many possible outcomes, rather than the ultimate sign of success, had a ripple effect: it allowed them to make decisions in a more holistic way. They encouraged their sons and daughters to play multiple sports, act in school plays, and participate in school government. Taking part in a wide range of activities may have had some negative repercussions, but the long-term benefits outweighed those costs. Leading balanced lives made them aware of the multitude of opportunities, both on and off the athletic field, that could bring them satisfaction in the future.

ACKNOWLEDGMENTS

This project began as a conversation more than ten years ago, when our children were in high school, playing soccer at different public high schools that had a long-standing healthy rivalry. We saw each other on the sidelines at games and talked on the Vassar campus, where we have been longtime colleagues. The more we talked, the more we recognized similarities in our experiences as parents navigating a youth sports world that was far less familiar than we had anticipated when we first signed up our kids to play in local soccer and baseball programs.

In deciding to study and write about youth sports, we knew right away that we needed to extend our knowledge beyond our own experiences as sports parents, and we have been fortunate to have had so many participants in the youth sports world generously share their time and their perspectives with us. We are deeply thankful to the many parents, players, youth coaches, referees, youth league administrators, and college coaches who sat down with us for interviews, answering our questions with interest and enthusiasm, sharing stories that led to new questions, and often pointing us toward others to interview. We hope future youth sports participants will benefit from what we learned from these rich and thoughtful interview responses. We also appreciate the coaches who permitted us to observe their teams and the many parents with whom we talked informally at practices, games, and tournaments over the years.

Particularly in the early stages of this project, we were fortunate to work with several exceptional research assistants. Thank you to Nyah Berg, Nick Hoynes, Zach Leazer, Neena McBaer, Colleen O'Connell, Tali Shapiro, and Lauren Wiebe, each of whom made a valuable contribution to the research for this book. Through the development of the prospectus for the book, Mary Beth Kilkelly, Andrew Meier, Hilary Jacobs, and Peter Stein provided valuable advice. As this project began to take shape as a book for a broad readership, beyond the academic audiences that have been our typical readers, we were fortunate to have the support and vision of our agent Linda Konner and the assistance of developmental editor Karen Chernyaev. We very much appreciate the team at Central Recovery Press, especially executive editor Valerie Killeen and acquisitions editor Nancy Schenck, for believing in this book and helping it to find the right audience. Finally, we could never have written this book without the support and patience of our families, to whom we are forever grateful.

ENDNOTES

Notes on Chapter One

1. National Federation of State High School Associations. 2023–24 High School Athletics Participation Survey. https://www.nfhs. org/media/7213111/2023-24-nfhs-participation-survey-full.pdf.

2. Jonathan Change (2020), "The Widening Accessibility Gap in Youth Sports."
   https://www.wbur.org/onlyagame/2020/06/26/otto-loewy-youth-sports-accessibility-gap.

3. *Hartford Courant,* "Connecticut Little League Forced to Adjust Amid Youth Baseball Participation Decline," July 10, 2019. https://www.courant.com/sports/hc-sp-little-league-youth-baseball-connecticut-participation-20190710-xq4b4trxdnehbbwodm4z35aulu-story.html.

4. Sean Gregory, "How Kids' Sports Became a $15 Billion Industry," *Time,* August 24, 2017. https://time.com/4913687/how-kids-sports-became-15-billion-industry/.

5. Research and Markets, "Youth Sports Market Projected to Reach $77.6 Billion by 2026 - Comprehensive Industry Analysis & Insights," December 26, 2019. https://www.globenewswire. com/news-release/2019/12/26/1964575/0/en/Youth-Sports-Market-Projected-to-Reach-77-6-Billion-by-2026-Comprehensive-Industry-Analysis-Insights.html.

6. N.A. Jayanthi, E.G. Post, T.C. Laury, and P.D. Fabricant, (2019), "Health Consequences of Youth Sport Specialization," *Journal of Athletic Training*, 54(10): 1040–49.

7. Jacob Bogage, "Youth sports study: Declining participation, rising costs, and unqualified coaches," *Washington Post,* 9/6/17.

Notes on Chapter Two

8. Family Education, "Rethinking Children's Play." Retrieved on 7/20/20 from: https://www.familyeducation.com/fun/games/rethinking-childrens-play.

Notes on Chapter Three

9. HALFF, "Youth and Amateur Sports Tourism Brings Economic Benefits to Local Economies," July 28, 2022. https://www.halff.com/news-insights/insights/youth-amateur-sports-tourism-brings-economic-benefits-local-economies//.

10. Research, *Athletic Insight: The Online Journal of Sport Psychology,* 8 (3): September 2006. https://www.researchgate.net/publication/43501311_Youth_Sports_Implementing_Findings_and_Moving_Forward_with_Research.

11. J. Fraser-Thomas and J. Côté, "Youth Sports: Implementing Findings and Moving Forward with Research," *Athletic Insight* 8 (3): 12–26, 2006.

12. National Federation of State High School Associations, Sports Medicine Advisory Committee. Sport Specialization Position Statement, April 2019. https://www.nfhs.org/media/1020399/sport-specialization-postion-statement-april-2019-final-copy.pdf.

13. J. Baker, S. Cobley, and J. Fraser-Thomas, "What Do We Know about Early Sport Specialization? Not Much!" *High Ability Studies,* 20 (1), 77–89, 2009. https://doi-org.libproxy.vassar.edu/10.1080/13598130902860507..

14. J. S. Brenner, M. LaBotz, D. Sugimoto, A. Stracciolini, "The Psychosocial Implications of Sport Specialization in Pediatric Athletes," *Journal of Athletic Training*, 54 (10):1021–29, October 2019. https://www.ncbi.nlm.nih.gov/pmc/articles/PMC6805069/.

15. Drew Watson, "Mental Health in Teen Athletes," Healthy Children.org., August 16, 2023. https://www.healthychildren.org/English/healthy-living/sports/Pages/mental-health-in-teen-athletes.aspx.

16. Bruce Kelley and Carl Carchia. "Hey, Data Data—Swing!"" ESPN, July 11, 2013. https://www.espn.com/espn/story/_/id/9469252/hidden-demographics-youth-sports-espn-magazine.

17. J. S. Brenner, M. LaBotz, D. Sugimoto, and A. Stracciolini, "The Psychosocial Implications of Sport Specialization in Pediatric Athletes," Journal of Athletic Training, 54 (10):1021–29, October 2019. https://www.ncbi.nlm.nih.gov/pmc/articles/PMC6805069/.

18. N. Jayanthi, C. Pinkham, L. Dugas, B. Patrick, C. Labella, "Sports Specialization in Young Athletes: Evidence-Based Recommendations," *Sports Health* 5(3):251–57, May 2013. https://pubmed.ncbi.nlm.nih.gov/24427397/.

19. N. Jayanthi, C. Pinkham, L. Dugas, B. Patrick, C. Labella, "Sports Specialization in Young Athletes: Evidence-Based Recommendations," *Sports Health* 5(3):251–57, May 2013. https://www.ncbi.nlm.nih.gov/pmc/articles/PMC3658407/.

20. National Sports Medicine Institute, "Sport Specialization in Young Athletes and Promoting Long-Term Athletic Development," The National Sports Medicine Institute, October 22, 2020. https://www.nationalsportsmed.com/sports-specialization/.

21. Robert M. Malina, "Early Sport Specialization: Roots, Effectiveness, Risks. Current Sports Medicine Reports," 9(6): 364–71, November 2010. DOI: 10.1249/JSR.0b013e3181fe3166. https://journals.lww.com/acsm-csmr/Fulltext/2010/11000/ Early_Sport_Specialization___Roots,_Effectiveness,.14. aspx.

22. J. S. Brenner; Council on Sports Medicine and Fitness, "Sports Specialization and Intensive Training in Young Athletes," *Pediatrics.* 138(3), September 2016. DOI: 10.1542/peds.2016-2148. https://pubmed.ncbi.nlm.nih. gov/27573090/.

23. N. A. Jayanthi, E. G. Post, T. C. Laury, and P. D. Fabricant, "Health Consequences of Youth Sport Specialization," *Journal of Athletic Training.* 54(10):1040–49, October 2019. DOI: 10.4085/1062-6050-380-18. https://pubmed.ncbi.nlm. nih.gov/31633420/.

24. N. Jayanthi, C. Pinkham, L. Dugas, B. Patrick, and C. LaBella, "Sports Specialization in Young Athletes: Evidence-Based Recommendations," *Sports Health* 5(3):251-7, May 2013. DOI:10.1177/1941738112464626. https://journals-sagepub-com.libproxy.vassar.edu/doi/10.1177/1941738112464626.

25. Drew Watson, "Mental Health in Teen Athletes," Healthy Children.org. August 16, 2023. https://www.healthychildren. org/English/healthy-living/sports/Pages/mental-health-in-teen-athletes.aspx.

26. Greigory Dimailig, American Psychiatric Association, "How to Recognize Depression and Anxiety in Young Athletes and How to Help," October 26, 2023. https://www.psychiatry. org/news-room/apa-blogs/depression-and-anxiety-in-young-athletes.

Notes on Chapter Four

27. ScholarshipStats.com.

28. NCSA, "Athletic Scholarships: Everything You Need to Know," https://www.ncsasports.org/recruiting/how-to-get-recruited/scholarship-facts.

29. ScholarshipStats.com.

Notes on Chapter Seven

30. Charlotte Faircloth, Intensive Parenting and the Expansion of Parenting, *Parenting Culture Studies*, E. Lee, J. Bristow, C. Faircloth, and J. Macvarish, eds. (London: Palgrave Macmillan, 2014), 25–50.

31. Sharon Hays, *The Cultural Contradictions of Motherhood* (Connecticut: Yale University Press, 1996).

32. Annette Lareau, *Unequal Childhoods,* second edition (Berkley, CA: University of California Press, 2011).

Notes on Chapter Eight

33. Erik Spanberg, "Youth Sports: Supply. Demand. Access.," *Sports Business Journal,* May 1, 2023. https://www.sportsbusinessjournal.com/Journal/Issues/2023/05/01/In-Depth/youth-sports.aspx.

34. Andrew W.Kuhn, Alan Z Grusky, Carsen R.Cash, Andre L. Churchwell, and Alex B. Diamond, "Disparities and Inequities in Youth Sports," *Current Sports Medicine Reports* 20(9):p 494–98, September 2021. https://journals.lww.com/acsm-csmr/fulltext/2021/09000/disparities_and_inequities_in_youth_sports.13.aspx.

35. Lindsey I. Black, Emily P. Terlizzi, and Anjel Vahratian, National Center for Health Statistics. Organized Sports Participation Among Children Aged 6–17 Years: United States, 2020, NCHS Data Brief, No. 441, August 2022. https://www.cdc.gov/nchs/data/databriefs/db441.pdf.

36. Women's Sports Foundation. https://www.womenssportsfoundation.org/.

37. Women's Sports Foundation, "Go Out and Play: Youth Sports in America," October 8, 2008. https://www.womenssportsfoundation.org/articles_and_report/go-out-and-play/.

Notes on Chapter Eleven

38. N. A. Jayanthi, E. G. Post, T. C. Laury, and P. D. Fabricant, "Health Consequences of Youth Sport Specialization," *Journal of Athletic Training,* 54(10) (2019): 1040–49.

A.S. Padaki, C. S. Ahmad, J. L. Hodgins, D. Kovacevic, T. S. Lynch, and C. A. Popkin, "Quantifying Parental Influence on Young Athlete Specialization: A Survey of Athletes' Parents," *Orthopedic Journal of Sports Medicine,* 5(9) (2017): 1–7.

A.S. Padaki, C. A. Popkin, J. L. Hodgins, D. Kovacevic, T. S. Lynch, and C. S. Ahmad, "Factors That Drive Youth Specialization," *Sports Health,* 9(6) (2017): 532–36.

E. Post, M. D. Rosenthal, and M. J. Rauh, "Attitudes and Beliefs Toward Sports Specialization, College Scholarships, and Financial Investment Among High School Baseball Parents," *Sports,* 7(12) (2019): 247.

39. Jonathan Haidt, *The Anxious Generation* (New York: Penguin Press, 2024).

40. Positive Coaching Solutions, www.positivecoach.com.

www.ingramcontent.com/pod-product-compliance
Lightning Source LLC
Chambersburg PA
CBHW022007080426
42733CB00007B/508